praise for *Heartsounds*

"Absorbing, wild, funny, tender... . . . An awesome and gripping book. It [is] about loving as much as about dying." —*The New York Times Book Review*

"If love, humor, and determination could restore a ruined heart, surely the Lears would have won." —*Cosmopolitan*

"Reads like a fine novel that has the additional resonance of truth." —*The Philadelphia Inquirer*

"[A] powerful and moving account of a man, a woman and an illness." —*The Dallas Morning News*

"A testament to the power of human love and the will to live!" —*Publishers Weekly*

"*Heartsounds* is a book that reads like a fine novel. . . . A rare, beautifully written cry against the modern ways of death, against death itself: It is worth every degree of the pain it takes to read it." —Joanne Greenberg, *Chicago Sun-Times*

"*Heartsounds*, a deeply felt account of a brave doctor's fight for a full life after a crippling heart attack, is both a celebration of an enviably good marriage and a cry of outrage—a book filled with love and honor and roaring against the night." —Mordecai Richler, *Book-of-the-Month Club News*

"It hurts, illuminates, loads the circuits with rage, transmits the energy of a great love . . . beautifully written!" —Gail Sheehy

"Exhilarating—thanks to Lear's proud honesty!"   —Gore Vidal

"It is *Love Story* made honest and life-size!"   —Ira Levin

"The most moving love story I have ever read." —Joanne Woodward

"Written from the heart . . . It has much to say about the human spirit. I can't imagine anyone reading this book without feeling the better for it."   —Norman Cousins

"No praise is too high for *Heartsounds*. . . . An extraordinary book . . . Martha has done a remarkable job balancing her love story with Hal, her desperate, angry struggle to save him, along with tough, specific reportage on the medical profession. . . . What a sense Martha has for anecdote, for character, for time and place . . . for *life*."   —Patricia Bosworth

"The most courageous book I have ever read . . . A brilliant, powerful love story."   —Nancy Friday

"This is so lusty, so passionate and powerful a love story, that it seems to stand up to death itself."   —Marlo Thomas

"A searing chronicle of grace under pressure . . . Readers may learn to make that ultimate toast with which Martha Lear concludes her book: *L'chaim*—to life."   —*The San Francisco Examiner*

"Engrossing, touching and very frightening . . . Martha Lear is an eloquent, powerful writer."   —Dr. William A. Nolen,
The Washington Post

"Unsparing, proud . . . One weeps through the last chapter."
—*Los Angeles Times*

"A deeply stirring book . . . Though the story is a familiar one, I have never before read it set down with such power and emotion."
—*John Barkham Reviews*

"A riveting account of life and love and, yes, death."
—*The Washington Star*

echoes of
heartsounds

echoes of heartsounds

a memoir

MARTHA WEINMAN LEAR

OPEN ROAD

INTEGRATED MEDIA

NEW YORK

Copyright © 2014 by Martha Weinman Lear

Cover design by Mauricio Díaz

978-1-4976-4615-5

Published in 2014 by Open Road Integrated Media, Inc.
345 Hudson Street
New York, NY 10014
www.openroadmedia.com

For GLORIA
and for SANDY—
both the best of the best

foreword

It was three decades ago, it was yesterday, when I sat by the bed of a much-beloved husband, a doctor who had become a patient overnight. He had suffered a massive heart attack, followed by severe and mysterious "complications," and died, after a long struggle, at the age of fifty-seven. In the book *Heartsounds*, I wrote about that marriage and that struggle.

Now my role had been reversed. Now I lay in a hospital bed recovering from a heart attack, followed by severe and mysterious "complications." Ghosts hovered all about me, for I was in the same hospital, the same cardiac unit, with the same attending doctor, as when Hal had lain in this place.

Foreword

But now another husband, also dearly loved, sat by my bedside, as I had sat by Hal's. Another husband wheeled me in my wheelchair through these same corridors where I had wheeled Hal. And amid these confusions, past and present began to merge as those ghosts kept pulling me back through time and space to that other bed, that other heart attack, that other marriage—that other life.

Two books, one new and one written long ago, tell the story of both of those lives. They are companion pieces. This new book, *Echoes of Heartsounds,* goes from the emotional storms and the challenges of widowhood to the astonishment of finding new love in my senior years, and on to the sudden cardiac crisis and the persistence of those ghosts that forced me, finally, to confront a past that I had never put wholly to rest.

The earlier book, *Heartsounds,* takes you into that past. It is the backstory, out of which everything followed. It describes the long medical odyssey through which a stricken doctor came to see medicine in a devastating new light; we both learned life-changing lessons about marriage, dependency, and love; and I was enabled, after he was gone, to move on to tomorrow.

echoes of
heartsounds

chapter one

It crept up on me like a cat burglar. No sound, no warning. A balmy late October afternoon, the trees along Central Park West showing the last pale traces of autumn color, dusk casting shadows in the kitchen where I sat at the butcher-block table, eating a bowl of soup and feeling totally, unremarkably well.

That was one moment. In the next, something was wrong. Something suddenly was there, inside me, something that did not belong there, that had never been there before, not painful but powerfully *there*, a strange unpleasant fluttering sensation low in my chest, down there at the sternum, like the fluttering of wings, fluttering upward now toward the collarbone. I stood and considered it.

As I ate, I had been making a list of clothes to pack for the birthday trip. This was our custom, one of the countless little customs that define a marriage, to take each other away on birthday trips. Mine were in March. Usually he took me south, to Caribbean islands ringed by waters of improbable beauty. His were in October. I took him north, to country inns awash in chintz, for the foliage, or to American cities we loved—San Francisco, Chicago, New Orleans. The next day, we were scheduled to fly to Charleston.

But now there was this foreign presence within me. The strange fluttering had grown stronger, those wings now insistently beating their way up into my throat. The room was warm, in fact a bit too warm, but suddenly I was ice-cold. I began to shake. A moment later, I felt nausea, everything coming suddenly, and now there was pain too, not great but pain, midline, Adam's apple down to sternum, and with this pain came a dreadful sense of foreboding.

I went into the bedroom, where he was packing. I said, "Al, something's the matter with me."

"What do you mean? What do you feel?"

"Nausea."

It grabbed hold of me just then, it clogged my throat, and I was caught up in a paroxysm of dry heaves. In moments, I was kneeling on the bathroom floor, clutching a pillow to my chest and retching into the toilet bowl, so violently that I felt I would spew out my life.

He stood helpless in the doorway. I said, in a moment's pause, "Do you think I could be having a heart attack?"

"Oh, of course not," he said. "You've got food poisoning." The soup? Surely not the soup, perfectly good soup, mushroom barley, I had made it just the day before, we'd eaten it at dinner, I'd refrigerated it overnight. "Or maybe it's some kind of stomach bug," he said.

He might be right. Still, I knew—I had read about it, and in fact, I had written about it—that heart attacks can present themselves very differently in women from the stereotypical ways they do in men. Women rarely suffer that cliché of the crushing pain, the elephant sitting on the chest, the sudden collapse. There may be no more than this clogging I felt in my throat, this modest pain in the chest, or maybe not even this much, maybe just a heaviness in the arm, the shoulder, the neck, something slight, almost a nonevent, a pale wind blowing through town and leaving no visible trail. Which was why it often goes undiagnosed.

I called my doctor's service. "Yes, it's urgent," I said. "I'm having pain in my chest."

He called back immediately. I reported symptoms: the fluttering, the pain, the chills, the shaking, the vomiting, and now diarrhea, too. He asked a rapid sequence of questions: *Do you have pain in your throat?* No. *Do you have shortness of breath?* No. *Any sweating?* No. *Turn on your left side. Does that make it worse?* No. *Now your right side. Is it worse?* No.

"Well," he said, "with the diarrhea, it doesn't sound like your heart. I can't say a thousand percent that it's not, but on the tiny chance that it could be, it doesn't seem necessary to go racing to the emergency room with the way you feel now. Just see it through and come in for an EKG in the morning."

The nausea eased. I said, "Maybe my anxiety is making the pain worse. I should take a tranquilizer."

"Good idea," my husband said. He knows me. He knows my anxieties that come from the weight of the genes: My mother and her mother, breast cancer, both breasts. My father and his father, and brother and uncles too, first coronaries in their fifties, dead in their sixties.

I sat on the edge of the bed, still hugging a pillow to my chest. He stood eying me, pretending more nonchalance than he felt. Within an hour, the pain stopped, the pill kicked in, and I slept.

I awoke feeling predictably washed out, but otherwise well. Perhaps it wasn't necessary to call for the EKG appointment? "You might as well. You told him you would," my husband said.

The doctor's receptionist said, "It's a crazy day, Mrs. Lear, but he told us to squeeze you in."

Every day was a crazy day and he always told them to squeeze me in. He was overworked, overburdened, his waiting room always SRO, but he made time for me. We had a bond that went way back, Stuart and I. Thirty years before, he had been the young doctor on call in the hospital emergency room the night I had brought in my first husband, my late husband, Harold Lear: a doctor who had suddenly become a patient with the onset of his first coronary four years earlier. That night in the ER was his eleventh emergency admission. He was on a downward trajectory and he knew it. Everyone knew it. He had come to that point at which doctors often pull back, close down, stop returning the telephone calls, become less attentive, not necessarily consciously and not because they are uncaring, but because they cannot bear to confront their own impotence in the face of the inevitable.

Six months later, Hal would be dead. For those six months, Stuart became his primary doctor. Medically, there was little more that could be done, but in the sheer caring part of medical care, there was plenty that could be done, and Stuart did it. He gave Hal attention, he gave him respect. At the end, there was great mutual affection, and at the memorial service, Stuart spoke, saluting the spirit of his near-indomitable patient; since then he had been my own primary doctor and the friend to whom, through the intervening years, I had remained deeply grateful.

"Want me to go to the appointment with you?" Al asked.

"No need. I'll be back soon."

"You think we'll be able to go to Charleston?"

"Of *course* we'll be able to go to Charleston!"

"You really feel okay?"

"Perfectly!" And I was out the door.

"Your cane!" he called.

My cane. A torn meniscus had been causing pain in my knee. "We could operate on it," the orthopedist had said, "but sometimes, when you have underlying arthritis"—as I had—"those surgeries aren't too successful. Try using a cane for six weeks, and then we'll reevaluate."

I hated using the cane. I hated the seventeen metaphors for *cane*, the nervous jokey preoccupation that we had all begun to show, my friends and I, with health, symptoms, doctors, aches, pains.

"When I was a young girl," Molly had told us, the Richmond lilt soft in her voice, "my mother would have her friends come to tea, and I would hear them, and all they ever talked about was doctors and sickness, and it was so *boring*. I swore that when I grew up, I would *never* do that." Pause. "But I didn't realize how much *fun* it would be."

We had all laughed. That particular laughter, with a tinge of rue.

I took the cane. In the street, waiting for a cab, I started playing with it, twirling it about my legs like a demented baton twirler, until the doorman said, "Watch it, ma'am, you could break a leg on that thing," after which I accepted that a cane is a cane and stood quietly until a cab pulled up to the curb.

When they saw what was going on inside me, one of them told me afterward, they thought it was quite remarkable, really, that I was feeling so unremarkably well.

chapter two

"You're not going to Charleston."

I had known it. I had been hoping that I didn't know it, but I had known it.

I had been waiting and hoping in the waiting room, a space filled, like every doctor's waiting room, with vibrations of hope and fear. It was always crowded, mostly with seniors. Stuart's patients adored him. Especially the very old ones, who had no one else to listen to their complaints. Especially the very sick ones, from whom other doctors may have distanced themselves; Stuart stuck around, as he had done with Hal.

I sat for some ten minutes, willing myself to be wrong. Then I was shown into Stuart's consulting room. ("You sure sound better than you did last night," he said. "Totally fine. We're going to Charleston this evening," I said), and then I went to the examining room for my electrocardiogram.

It was done quickly. "Okay, you can get dressed," the nurse said and took the printout to show the doctor.

She returned almost immediately.

"Stop dressing."

"Why?"

"He wants to do an echocardiogram."

"Why?"

She shrugged. "Maybe he sees some change." Red flags waving in her eyes.

And now here is Stuart, looking stricken. "You're not going to Charleston," he says.

I am on the examining table, half-dressed. "Why not?"

"Something's happened."

"What?"

"Not sure yet."

But clearly he is sure. His face is grim, as I have never seen it before; his mouth is set in a thin grim line and I can sense, rather than see, his teeth clenched hard behind those lips. He is muttering, more to himself than to me, "I can't believe it . . . The diarrhea last night . . . That just didn't fit the picture . . . I should have . . . I could kick myself . . ."

Stuart has always expressed faith in my long and healthy future. For twenty-odd years he has been monitoring my annual flu, my encroaching arthritis, my bad cholesterol ("not *too* bad"), my good cholesterol ("*excellent*"), the very texture of my platelets ("beautiful!"), and, whenever he would listen to my heart, he would punctuate his faith with a *tch* of pleased disbelief and the invariable assurance, "You've got the heart of a teenage kid! You'll outlive us all."

Oh, Doctor. Where is your faith now? He is doing the echo and I am looking at him and he is looking at the screen and he looks vastly different from the composed man I saw five minutes ago. He is agitated. He is miserable. Come on, Stuart. Me, Martha? A heart attack? Don't be silly. I know it, but I know it merely on the level of objective reality, the level of mere facts. *Subjectively*, where we live most of our emotional lives, where feelings trump facts every time, I know no such thing. I reject it completely, Stuart. Something happened, sure, something happens all the time, but *to other people*. You've got the wrong electrocardiogram. You've got the wrong diagnosis. You've got the wrong I don't know what, but it's wrong.

But wait. Now that I think back, I remember—how odd that I didn't remember this earlier, last night, this morning—that I have been feeling unspecifically unwell for weeks, a generalized blah, saying often to Al, "Do I look awfully pale?" and "I just don't feel great," and "Why am I so *tired* all the time?" So why is it such a shock to hear that *something happened?*

Into a thick silence, I ask now: "Is it mild?"

"Not mild," he says. *Not mild.* That is all he says, and instantly I am off on a thirty-year-old trip. I am on a story assignment in France and have just gotten word that Dr. Harold Lear is lying in a bed in the Coronary Care Unit of his hospital, where he is on staff, in New York City, having suffered a heart attack, and now I am screaming into the telephone, for the transatlantic connection is dreadful, "*Mild?* Did you say "*mild?*" and an unknown doctor's voice screams back, "Not *mild. Myo.* A massive myocardial infarction . . ."

Oh Jesus. The terror of that moment. It comes back to me like a poisonous taste. And here now, in this absurdly unbelievable moment of my own, here is Stuart saying, "Not mild." *A massive myocardial infarction . . .*

"Is it massive, then?" Coming into the Coronary Care Unit

where he lay in a cubicle, kneeling at his bedside, hearing him whisper *It will be alright; it will be just like it was*, sweet deceitful lies, for as the doctor knows, as even I know, nothing is likely to be just like it was ever again.

And Stuart says now, "Not massive. Moderate."

Moderate. A new word for a new phase: all things in moderation.

"I am stunned," I say.

"So am I."

"I can't believe it."

"Neither can I." He still looks stricken. I learn much later, after I have done the research, that diarrhea almost never accompanies a heart attack. This was an easy one to miss. Any doctor might have missed it, even the best, and Stuart is the best, and knows it. None of which, at this moment, keeps him from looking stricken.

"What happens now?"

"I'm going to admit you. We'll send for an ambulance."

"I don't need an ambulance; I can take a cab." More echoes of Hal: "I don't need a stretcher; I can walk." This the day before he died. Walking dazed, his final walk, in his blue terrycloth robe, through the lobby of our building, refusing the doorman's arm, staggering out to the street and into the waiting ambulance.

Now I wait for my ambulance. They seat me in the corridor, away from other patients. Why? Am I contagious? Well, yes, I suppose I am, in a way: the irrepressible contagiousness of bad news.

A heart attack. Fancy that. If they had told me I had breast cancer, I would have said, "Of course, no surprise there: consider the genes." If they had told me I had terminal lung cancer, I would have been devastated but not in the least surprised. I would have said, "What took it so long to show up?" For I had smoked two to three packs a day for forty years, and after quitting—a triumph, hard won—it had became a waiting game. While other people, stricken in various ways, might say, "Why me?" I kept saying, "Why *not* me?" thanking the gods for my luck thus far and waiting for the luck to run out. Cigarettes will ruin a heart even faster than they ruin a lung, I knew that. But I had never expected the luck to run out on *my* heart. I am not certain why. Perhaps because, mere facts to the contrary (fact: heart disease is the number one killer of American women), and my own knowledge to the contrary (for I have written many articles about medical matters, I should know better than to think stereotypically), there still exists that knee-jerk assumption that coronaries are what happen to *men*.

Okay, what must I do now? I know very well what I must

do, but I don't want to do it. What I must do now is call my husband and tell him that I am sorry to spoil his birthday, but we can't go to Charleston because I have had . . . how to put this . . . a heart attack? How do I put this to a man who, some twelve years ago, which in its own way is ten minutes ago, awoke in the middle of the night to find his wife—his first, late wife, his wife of nearly forty years—dead on the bedroom floor?

My cell phone does not seem to be working. Its workings are beyond me. We are both, Al and I, technologically challenged, a harmonious meshing of incompetencies.

Someone hands me a landline phone.

Al answers: "Hello?"

"Hi."

"Well? What did Stuart say?"

"He said . . . Al? We can't go to Charleston."

Warily: "Why not?"

"Listen, Al."

"I'm listening."

"I had a heart attack."

"You're kidding."

He knows that I am not kidding. I would be crying, except that I don't believe it yet. You can't cry over what you don't believe. There is silence while we breathe in emanations of each other's disbelief.

"Where are you now?"

"In Stuart's office. I'm waiting for the ambulance."

"Okay. I'll meet you at the hospital." Cool voice. What does this cost him? Is he in a shocked state of mind? Is he in a hyperactive state of mind, looking down a long dark road, imagining a second widowerhood? Or, far worse, imagining life with a cardiac invalid, pushing her in her wheelchair, portable oxygen tank in her desiccated lap, across the many cobblestones of life? Imagining what else?

Stuart's staff, four or five of them, now stand in a semi-circle gazing at me, but they maintain a curious distance, as though standing on the far side of the floral arrangements, gazing at the bier.

The EMTs arrive. There are three of them. One is a Hasidic Jew, full regalia, black coated, Santa Claus bearded, very merry. "Do you have pain?" he asks, as in "Do you like candy?" And, yes, I now have some pain again. He says, "Lift your tongue," and gives three squirts of nitroglycerin, like a breath freshener. "Better?" He grins at me. Meanwhile, the other two are loosening my clothes, attaching wires, discs, who knows what. A moment later: "Still got pain?" I nod. "We fix it! Lift your tongue," says my merry Hasid.

Now they are strapping me into a contraption that converts from a chair to a gurney. They begin to wheel me out. The staff still stands motionless, eyeing me nervously, and still at that curious distance. "Good luck, Mrs. Lear," one says. "You'll be fine."

We are out through the lobby and into the street. Passersby politely avert their gazes, in the correct New York way. I am hoisted into the ambulance. I hate ambulance sirens. I have hated them ever since one went wailing through the night as I sat inside, crying, "Daddy, don't die! Listen to me! Don't die!" into the face of my dead father, who had collapsed in the midst of my brother's wedding reception. And now the cursed wail would be for me. *Let me out of here! This is all a mistake!* But the doors are closing, with my merry Hasid on the outside, saying, "Bye-bye, you'll be okay."

"No, I want you to come with me," I cry, for by this time I love him, I love his good cheer, he is my amulet.

"I can't," he says. "I'm already late for my dental appointment," and begins to run off, the long coattails flapping. Suddenly, he turns. One last grin. "You'll be hotsy-totsy!" he says. "But maybe you shouldn't run in the Marathon."

It was the first of many jokes I would hear from many doctors about not running in the Marathon.

chapter three

In the emergency room, I was immediately surrounded by doctors and nurses. It is always like that in emergency rooms. You can sit for hours cradling your broken arm, your roiling belly, your bleeding scalp, but show up with any suspicion of a heart attack and they get to you fast. The phrase *chest pain* is equivalent to *Open Sesame* in emergency rooms, with urgent reason: half of all coronary victims, unattended, die within the first thirty minutes.

They began working on me with that fierce cool concentration of well-oiled emergency teams, yet with courtesy, with a comforting show of awareness that this body, upon which they were applying discs and tourniquets, into which they were sticking needles and tubes, out of which they were drawing blood, belonged to a real live humanoid. They introduced themselves. They said, "How do you feel?" and "Don't worry, we're taking care of everything," and "You're going to be okay," and I thought, Oh, this is interesting, this is some difference from all those years ago in this very same hospital, in this same emergency room, when they worked on Hal like automatons, silent, nameless, expressionless, working not upon a person but upon a failing body part. They must be teaching bedside manners in medical schools these days. (And, in fact, they are. They have to. Competition has forced hospitals to improve their manners.)

One of the team surrounding me, perhaps its leader, was telling me something about pictures. They wanted to take pictures. X-rays of my heart, a procedure called "coronary angiography," which meant . . .

I knew what it meant. I remembered when Hal had explained to me—after the fact, because he knew that I would have been terrified for him if he had told me beforehand—how it was done. How a catheter is inserted into the femoral artery, down there at the groin, and slowly, painstakingly, threaded all the way up into the arteries of the heart—by many measures of travel, an awesome distance; and how dye is then injected into those arteries to show where the blockages may be—the blockages, the plaque, testament to years of living and smoking and, of course, the genes. And the tricky part, he explained—again, after the fact—is to inject precisely the right amount of dye at precisely the right speed, so that blood can keep flowing through the artery at the same time as the dye. Because if they don't inject enough, they don't get good pictures. And if they inject too much it may fill the artery, plug it up, leaving no room for the blood to flow through, which would be functionally the same as having a heart attack, and the patient may die.

"Too much dye, I die," he had said to me, making a little joke of it—after the fact.

The doctor was explaining now that if this procedure revealed a blocked artery, the surgeon might decide to embed a stent, a small mesh metal tube, to keep the artery open. In my befogged mind, this was a troubling idea. A foreign object in my heart? There were of course other foreign objects embedded in me, my mouth was full of them, inlays, dental bridges, countless fillings in cavities acquired over the decades. In a mouth they were acceptable, a tongue soon made them feel at home. But in a *heart* . . . We may know rationally that the soul of the self is in the brain, but our literature, our poetry, our pop songs, our clichés, our most enduring myths locate that self insistently and lovingly—warm heart, cold heart, faint heart, pure heart, hard heart, tender heart, stout heart, aching heart, heart's desire, heart's delight, heart's ease, heart to heart, heart of hearts, Peg O' My Heart—in the heart. A small mesh metal tube spoils the picture.

I needed to know, the doctor was saying, that coronary angiography involved possible complications. There were risk factors. He enumerated the risk factors: (1) bleeding; (2) infection; (3) another heart attack; (4) death.

"But we think," he said, "that the benefit outweighs the risks."

Given these possible complications, they would require me to sign a consent form.

I thought about this. My thinking may have been muddled, but at the time it seemed transparently clear. I thought how it had been in Hal's day, almost three decades earlier, when coronary angiography was relatively new. He had told me—after the fact—that mortality rates were high, and shockingly high—35 percent—when the procedure was performed within six weeks after a heart attack.

The procedure had been performed upon him four weeks after a heart attack.

And here I am, I thought, one day after a heart attack.

This is not what you would call good timing.

Oh, but listen: That was then. This is now. Time marches, techniques improve. The surgical techniques they used back then are probably antediluvian today. You have to be told about the risks, informed consent requires that they tell you, but surely the risks are minimal now.

In the midst of this conference with myself, a woman, a nurse or an aide, touched my arm, bent toward me, and said softly, "I'll pray for you," and left the cubicle.

Hold on. Let us consider. Would she have said that if the risks were minimal now?

Pray for me, will she? I myself pray to no deity, but I'll take all the help I can get. They always said that what carried Rose Kennedy through her odyssey of grief, when she lost those golden boys, was the force of her religious faith. In such circumstances, Catholics clearly have a leg up. As in that sweet, tuneful ode to optimism, Don't know where or when but they know they'll meet again some sunny day . . . Yes, that is one hell of a leg up. As for Protestants, I can't say. I haven't the information. The promise of heavenly reward may vary from sect to sect. But I do know that Jews don't do too well in this particular. An afterlife may be available, but the details are murky, there are no firm guarantees, the holy texts leave room for disagreement; it is not the sort of setup that allows persons of the Hebrew faith, and certainly not those of us who are short on faith, to count absolutely, beyond question or nagging doubt, upon any celestial alumni reunions.

So death, really, would be a very serious complication.

Still: *The benefit outweighs the risks.*

Also: *They must know what they're doing.*

The latter thought was comforting, although untrue— I knew better, having been married to a doctor, having moved in circles of doctors, having learned that doctors, even the best of them, do not always and necessarily know what they are doing. Even so, the thought was comforting, as clichés often are, simply by virtue of their familiarity. The linguistic equivalent of old shoes. *They must know what they're doing.* It is the ultimate security blanket. It is what allows us, finally, to relinquish control of ourselves: I am the sick one; they are the caretakers. So here, I'll give them my body, let them take care of it. I won't worry about it. Let *them* worry about it.

With this line of reasoning, the memory of my father's favorite joke popped out of the neuronal depths. Daughter has a date. Mommy says, "Don't let him kiss you, don't let him touch you, because Mommy will worry. And if he tries to get on top of you, you get on top of him instead. Let *his* mommy worry."

Oh, Daddy. I saw him clearly as he told his foolish little joke to a friend who was visiting him in the hospital, soon after his first heart attack. I laughed and heard someone say, "What's so funny?" I shook my head. It was too silly. It was too serious.

I recalled that sense of calm with which Hal, hospitalized after his own first coronary, had given himself over to the care of others. For a doctor to surrender control of a case is always hard, and never harder than when he himself is the patient. I had been surprised by the ease with which a medical man, so accustomed, as they all are, to exercising absolute authority, had relinquished it.

At the time I had been interviewing him almost daily, making notes for a book that would be called *Heartsounds*. Describing this sense of surrender, he had told me, as I later wrote:

". . . Of course he felt wary. But not greatly agitated. It was out of his hands, after all. He was no longer in charge. Other people were in charge. He could lie back now, aware that whatever they could do was being done and hoping that it was enough. It felt quite pleasant, really. No responsibility, no decisions to make. Nothing seemed crucial. Nothing could get close enough to seem crucial. If they had come to him and said, 'Sir, there is war. There are bombs. There is plague. We must evacuate,' he would have told them, 'I don't work here. Don't bother me. Do not disturb.' He felt helpless and at peace.

"Later he would have to resume responsibility . . . But he didn't want to think about it yet. There was no need to do anything—anything at all; simply to float here cocooned in this soft postcardiac calm, observing how curious this familiar world looked from his new vantage point. . . ."

This agreeable complaisance, which had puzzled me then, I understood very well now as I lay in the emergency room. *Simply to float here cocooned in this soft postcardiac calm* . . . Exactly!

I signed the consent form.

They all wished me well—not prayerfully, for which I was grateful, but simply as we say, "Have a good trip" to a traveler boarding a plane—and I was wheeled upstairs to the catheterization lab.

It's cold in here. Why do operating rooms and catheterization rooms and MRI rooms and CAT scan rooms always feel like refrigerators? It is enough to set off tremors, as though I am frightened. Which I am not. They are doing things to me. I believe they are hooking me up to a drip. Somebody says, "You'll be awake, but you'll feel sort of woozy." In fact, I already feel sort of woozy. Maybe they slipped me a little something in the emergency room, to get the ball rolling. A masked man approaches me. He says, "Hello, Mrs. Lear, I'm Dr. Kay. I'll be doing this procedure." I tell him *How do you do.* It's all quite chummy, as in the ER, and again I marvel at the difference between now and back then. No, not simply the difference; it's the antithesis. Back then they were taught to depersonalize. Now they are taught to personalize. *What's this?* A length of fabric, blue or green, lightweight but opaque, has now been draped in such a way that it obscures my vision. I ask, "Will I be able to watch the screen?" Someone says, "No, you won't." This is a disappointment. What had made the experience so incredible—*incredible!* Hal had said—had been watching on the television monitor as the catheter had traveled that stupefying distance from his femoral artery to his heart. He had lain there and followed its progress, seeing it climb ever so slowly—slo-mo, we would say today—up behind his bladder, creeping above the small of his spine, snaking upward along the back of his belly, behind his intestines, then up between his kidneys, and watched awestruck as it snaked through an opening in his diaphragm and into his chest cavity. "I thought, my God, this is my heart. I am looking at the inside of my heart. That is my own heart, beating, contracting and expanding, up there on the television screen. You know what it was like?" he said. "Like God suddenly making an appearance." Some trip. Well, if the thing must be done, at least, I thought, I would have my own incredible experience. But no. I cannot watch. This is unfair. I push: "Why *can't* I watch the screen?" Nobody answers. A sensation of wetness, down there at the groin. I know what that is. They are painting me with antiseptic. That stuff is usually mustard colored. My least favorite color. And it's tenacious stuff, as Hal found. Doesn't easily wash off. Ugh. Someone—the masked man?—says, "You'll feel some pressure now." I feel it, a little. Then a release, and then pressure again, harder this time, but still nothing to get nervous about. I am waiting to get nervous about something else. The heat. A nurse warned Hal about the heat, that he would have the sudden sensation of tremendous heat, followed by the sensation that he was about to die. After angiography, the patients all had those complaints, she said. The heat was a flushing sensation, very strong. It came from the injection of dye. The feeling that they were about to die came because when the dye was injected, the heart was getting less oxygen. It could cause great pain, like a heart attack. *Too much dye, I die.* But the feeling would pass quickly, she said. That's good. Hal said afterward that it had been a terrific flush, as though his body had been shoved into an oven, but not scary, because he expected it. But the other thing had been deeply scary. Sudden massive pain in his chest, terrible total ebbing of strength, dread, foreboding, *is this it?* But within moments, the pain had lessened, he had felt the rapture of relief, and then the heat had begun to ease too, it had begun retreating in waves downward through his body, and he had been left finally, he said, with a powerful burning sensation in his anus. "And that was how it ended—with a pain in the ass." I seem to be floating now in a sort of twilight zone, hearing voices, muted, as though through an open window on a summer night. I was just thinking that I may have to worry about worries that didn't exist for Hal. What was I thinking? Oh, yes, the stent. If they put that stent thing, that thing that is made of mesh metal, if they put that thing into me, will I set off bells in airports? If I travel. If I am ever well enough to travel again. Hal never was. Softly, softly, now, I hear a voice say, "Good. Good," and then, "You may feel a little heat now." Okay, here we go, the heat. I brace for it, but it does not come. Why not? Possibly they're using a better-quality dye these days. But wait, there is no feeling that I am about to die, either. The nurse said they *always* complain about that. Where is the feeling that I am about to die? Is there some mistake here? Could they be doing the wrong procedure on me? That happens. (No, no, Doctor, you were supposed to take out the *left* kidney.) Do they think I am somebody else? That happens, too. The wrong ID bracelet on the wrong wrist . . . Hello? Operator? Who am I? Is this a wrong number? Are the wires crossed? This is not a good connection. Can you hear me? Operator, listen, *don't disconnect me* . . . I need to know what is going on. I need reassurance. I need to hear a familiar voice. I need protection in this situation with these people who do not *necessarily* know what they are doing. Where the hell is my husband? Al would know what to do. He would be my . . . What do you call that person, that person in the hospital who protects your interests? I can't think of the word, I'm so close, it's right here on the tip of my tongue . . .

It seemed crucial to find the word. I thought it began with "om," but I was sinking deeper now into the twilight zone, *ommm . . . ommm . . .* and when I awoke, they were done.

chapter four

The telephone call had stunned him. Of course, people are always stunned by such news. But she had seemed so *well.* No sign of the previous night's distress. Setting off just this morning for the doctor's office, giving him such a cheery "So long, see you later." . . .

"Want me to go with you?" he had asked.

"No, why should you?"

"You think we'll be able to go to Charleston?"

"Of *course* we'll be able to go to Charleston!"

And then the telephone call. It had come—what?—just two hours ago? Three hours ago? How the world turns.

"We can't go to Charleston," she had said, which meant that it was serious, but who could have imagined *how* serious? Serious could mean an ulcer, a bacterial infection, a parasitic disease. Serious, in the dailyness of things, did not extend to life-threatening events.

Heart attack. Game-changing words. So shockingly out of nowhere. They had been married almost eight years now ("or almost two years, depending on your point of view," she enjoyed telling people, for they had been married on Leap Year Day—a frolic, a gesture, to indicate that they didn't really *need* the ceremony), and over those years she had had her complaints, mostly arthritis, not severe but worsening, as it had occurred with her mother ("Live long enough, and we women all become our mothers"—she liked saying that, too), but never anything serious. Never the least hint of anything serious. That was the astonishment: out of *nowhere.* Of course, that was what survivors always said: It came out of nowhere.

Last night, when she had knelt on the bathroom floor vomiting her heart (her *heart!*) out, and asked, "Do you think I could be having a heart attack?" he had assumed that she was overreacting to what was surely no more than a bad case of food poisoning, or what people always called a stomach bug, whatever that meant. His own notions of heart attacks demanded larger, more dramatic spectacles: clutching the chest, grimacing in agony, collapsing into unconsciousness, the whole silent-film panoply. He would not in a million years have thought that she might be right. But then, she knew more than he about medical matters. She had written often about medical subjects; she had done the research.

Immediately after the call, he had started thinking, *What should I do? First thing, stay calm. Next, get to where she is.* But she had said something about canceling the trip. Calling the airline, explaining the circumstance, canceling the trip. She had sounded totally collected, normal, not in any kind of panic. Which had been good for him, kept him from panic.

So he had called the airline. The clerk had been solicitous. "Don't you worry, Mr. Ruben. I'm sure she'll be all right." He had wanted to say, "What makes you sure?" He had thought how bizarre it was, that strangers offer assurances about matters of which they know absolutely nothing, and even more bizarre that we take comfort from their assurances.

Then he had telephoned his daughter, Julie, who lived nearby. He cut into the predictable exclamations of shock. "But it must have been a very mild attack," he said. "She sounded totally fine when she called."

Julie and Al, partners in grief when her mother, his wife, had died in such a sudden and devastating way. That one had not come from nowhere. That one had come from many bad directions. Many signs, many damaged body parts. You know what the possibilities are, you know and you know and you know, and yet, when it happens, there is always that incomprehensible surprise.

Judy, age sixty-five, had breast cancer. She had a radical mastectomy. For many years she had suffered severe breathing problems, for which she used an inhaler. "Was she a heavy smoker?" I had asked Al once. "Oh, yeah. Heavy." "When did she quit?" "Never. She cut down, but she never quit. She was sneaking cigarettes right up to the time she died."(Shades of Hal. Swearing repeatedly that *of course* he had quit, and going out for his daily walk, when he had hardly strength to walk at all, to pick stained butts out of the gutter and smoke them in secret and in shame.) Then she developed double vision. It was diagnosed as a tumor behind the eye—benign but crowding in, the thing had to be removed.

"They treated it with radiation, twice a week. And she would go from the radiation treatment directly to her office. She was some trouper, Judy. . . . When those treatments ended, she seemed well. A little weak, but basically well. That was how she seemed to me. And then, one night, not too long after the radiation was finished, we went to a concert at Lincoln Center. Then we came home and went to bed. And I got up in the middle of the night to go to the bathroom . . ." Voice faltering now, eyes peering into the void. ". . . and Judy was lying on the floor. I couldn't wake her. I tried and tried. I called 911. They walked me through doing CPR. I did mouth-to-mouth, I did chest compression. It was no good. Then the fire department came and tried to revive her, but it was still no good. End of story."

And then the bitter coda, having to call Julie and David, his son. That had been, he said, the worst task of his life. Julie had been living in San Francisco then. For her, the call had come at two A.M., for David, who lived outside Boston, at five A.M. To both of them, he said, "Mom died," not knowing how to soften the blow, and David had recognized, in what he described as his father's otherworldly tone, the sound of a man in shock.

So I had wondered, telephoning him, whether my own news might take him back to those harsh memories. How could it not? Here we go again, one wife gone, another going, going . . .

"Were you thinking of that?" I asked him, much later. "Were you wondering if you were going to be widowed again?"

"Not for a moment."

"Why not?"

"Because I never for a moment thought that you would die."

Not that he is an optimist, Al, but in this, as in all else, he was implacably realistic. The woman who had said, "We're not going to Charleston," and had asked him to call the airline and cancel the reservation—that could not have been a dying woman.

He sat in the waiting room outside the catheterization lab for what seemed like a terribly long time. Finally, the surgeon came and beckoned him into the corridor. The surgeon explained to him how one of the coronary arteries had closed completely, but then had opened again—which was a good sign, he said—illustrating it by closing and opening his fist, and that he had then put a stent in there to keep the artery open. And everything had gone well and his wife would be fine, she would be able to lead a normal life.

The door to the cath lab opened and Martha was wheeled

out. There was just a moment's glimpse before the gurney rolled on, but it was enough. She saw him and smiled. He thought, *But she* does *seem fine! How can this be someone who had a heart attack last night?*

He was still marveling at it when his daughter, Julie, arrived. "I just saw her," he said. "She smiled at me. She looked . . . *jaunty.*" Later, he often used that word, *jaunty*—it was so improbably the right word, he felt—when he was telling family and friends what had happened, how she had smiled and sounded, how amazed he had been to think that she had just come out of surgery.

A nurse came and said that they could visit the patient now. They were led into the recovery area, an alignment of open-fronted cubicles, and in each cubicle a figure lying prone upon a bed, and in several, visitors standing in solemn attitudes around the bed, as though arranged by someone with a camera, and all through this space there was a sort of holy hush, an aura of preparation for mourning, or prayer for redemption.

They came finally to her cubicle. She was propped high against pillows. She smiled now, not a small fleeting smile, as when he had seen her wheeled out of the catheterization lab, but a big full joyous grin, and into the foreboding silence of this place she said, "Hi, cookie."

He laughed aloud. *Cookie.* It was a fond moniker she bestowed upon friends and family, often upon himself, and he was well accustomed to hearing it. But to hear it at this moment, in this setting, was the best sign he could ever have asked for: She was truly okay.

She was perhaps *too* okay. She would not stop talking. She said that she must look awful. (In fact, he and Julie agreed that she looked remarkably healthy.) She said that her hair must be a mess. She said that she felt fine. She said that it was ridiculous to think that she'd had a heart attack. She started jabbering on about the *soup*, going on and on about the *soup*, the mushroom barley soup that she had made and they had eaten for dinner, no problem afterward, and she had refrigerated it overnight and eaten it again yesterday and soon thereafter had gotten so sick—a coronary, of all things!—and surely the soup was not to blame, her heart was to blame, but please, she said, just in case, please *do not eat the soup*.

"Easy," he said. "Don't talk so much. Don't get too excited." But she would not let up.

She gave him names to call. Her stepdaughter, her brother, a few close friends. Tell them what happened. But nobody else, she said.

"What do you mean? Other people will need to know."

"Not about the heart attack."

"Why not, Martha?"

"Because. Why does everyone have to know? I feel fine."

He didn't press it further.

They left soon after. He said, "Didn't she seem *jaunty*?"

At the nurses' station, someone in a white coat said that she would be discharged within a couple of days.

It was a Wednesday. She would be home, then, by the weekend. He was elated. He was not a man to say "Thank God," but he thought, *My God,* "Hi, cookie"? *Well, then, it's over. Everything is going to be all right.*

chapter five

It was dark but for a narrow shaft of light pushing through a partially open doorway. Dimly, in the wall to my right, I could see what appeared to be a window. It was dark out there, too. So this was nighttime, and clearly I was no longer in the recovery room, where there had been no doors.

I remembered then: this was a proper hospital room. It was in an area of the hospital called the Cardiac Unit. I was in this room not because I was sick—I did not feel in the least sick—but because of my absurd new reality.

My absurd new reality: I am now a cardiac. For someone who has always been abundantly healthy, this is preposterous. It is not a designation that goes away, as bronchitis, say, comes and runs its course and goes away. No, this is a designation I am stuck with for the rest of my life. (How long will that be? What are the statistics? How long, on average, do first-time cardiacs live? I must ask Stuart these questions, although I know that doctors hate the statistical-averages questions, which they call the "up-against-the-wall questions"). It is like the boozer who stops boozing: Once an alcoholic, always an alcoholic. Once a cardiac, always a cardiac.

Alcoholics cannot drink. Not ever. What can cardiacs not do?

Can I not eat red meat? What about ice cream? Sheer fat, after all, coating the artery walls, impeding the flow of blood, clogging the works, causing a perfectly healthy person to suffer the absurdity of a cardiac condition.

Can I not fly? Perhaps there is something about the pressures, thirty thousand feet up, the pressures in the chest and the outer, atmospheric pressures, coming into some inefficacious imbalance.

Can I not ski? What a pity. I have not skied in years, and no longer want to, but that is not the point. Can I not run in the Marathon? Boo hoo. Not that I ever have run it, not that I ever had the remotest desire to do so, but that is not the point either. The point is: I want to know the full range of my deprivations. A little self-pity is good for the heart.

Can I not be of good cheer? The few reformed alcoholics I have known—when they went dry—became depressed. Every one of them. Is this inevitable? I would not want to become depressed. Disgruntled is okay, but not depressed.

Can I not get excited? That's what they always say to cardiacs: don't get too excited. There is that ancient medical joke for the occasion, favored especially by cardiologists:

Recovering cardiac: Can I have sex, Doc?
Doctor: Yes, but only with your wife. I don't want you to get too excited.

"Easy." That was what Al said to me. "Don't get so excited. Don't talk so much." That was when he came with Julie. How long ago—an hour, a day, several days?—I have no idea.

Excited? I had been manic. I had been manic because I had not died from too much dye. I had been manic because I was feeling dandy. I had been manic because I had wanted to impress upon my husband the crucial importance of not letting everyone know that I was a cardiac.

Al had not understood this. I didn't fully understand it

myself. Nor was I proud of it, nor had I wanted to try to explain it.

It went back to the cultural tics of my childhood, when debilitating disease—heart failure, cancer, dementia—was somehow a shame, a shadow cast over the pride and competence of families, a secret to be kept in the back rooms of family life. ("Grandma has a bad memory," our mothers said with a smile and a shrug, making it sound like a bad cold.)

All that might be long gone, but I had been weaned on it and a spore of it festered in me. I did not want everyone—meaning everyone in our work and play circles—to know that I had had a heart attack, because they might be inclined to avoid me. They might feel that I could no longer work as hard, or play as merrily. They might be right.

I had seen it happen with Hal: how the illness of the body can do bad things to the soul—breed insecurity, depression, chronic anxiety—none of which brings much to the party. In *Heartsounds* I wrote, silently addressing his doctors: "You perhaps do not know from within how sickness humbles—how it clouds and corrodes and befouls the sense of self. I do not know why this should be so, that physical disease plays such cruel vanishing tricks upon the ego, even the sturdiest ego, given time enough. But I have seen it happen here, to this fine strong man, and I have read a bit about such things and I know that this is classic in long chronic disease, this is what the failures of the body do unerringly to the soul . . ."

And I myself had never had the sturdiest of egos, and this was what I feared now as much as I feared any assault upon my body, that this sickness of my heart might shred my self-regard. And so this vulnerability had to be kept closeted, lest the world find out.

There was also the psychology of the disease. Friends might want to maintain safe distance from something that was highly infectious—not the disease itself but its vibrations: There but for the grace, etcetera. People are not necessarily conscious of such feelings. The feet simply do the walking, toward or away.

I had not wanted to explain any of this to Al because he would have said, "Oh, Martha. That's ridiculous."

Maybe yes, maybe no.

The door opened wide. A light went on. A nurse said, "Good morning, Mrs. Lear. How are you feeling?"

"What time is it?"

"Almost six. How are you feeling?"

"How long have I been here?"

"Since last night. So how are we feeling this morning?"

I hated the *we*. I remembered in living color the time a private nurse said to Hal, "Have we made our pee-pee yet?" and he, in murderous impotent rage, had growled to me, "Get her the fuck out of here." But this nurse had a warm smile, which neutralized the *we*. "I'm feeling fine," I said.

"That's what we like to hear," she said. "I have some pills for you." And she proceeded to dole them out in little paper cups, naming each one: "And here is your Crestor, for cholesterol. And this is your Plavix, your blood thinner, this one is *very* important, and you must remember to take it every day, with this baby aspirin. Now, here is your famotidine . . ."

The full count was eight pills, two of which I was to take twice a day. How could I possibly remember? I'd been a one-pill user for some time—one of those anti-bone-loss pills that were endlessly flacked on television by postmenopausal actresses. Then, in the classic way of pharmacological research, some study had reported nasty long-term effects, and the doctor who had told me to start taking that pill told me to stop taking it, and I had stopped, cursing the way yesterday's panacea so often turned out to be tomorrow's poison. Then I had been started on a high-cholesterol pill, which had caused me, and apparently millions of other users, to have severe leg cramps, and which had not, as was now clear, kept me from the absurdity of my new condition.

Eight different pills!

"Forever?" I asked.

"You'll have to ask your doctor about that," the nurse said, and proceeded to take my blood pressure, for which I would now be taking a pill.

I said, "None of this seems real."

"Yes, that's what people always say," she said. "There is that process of denial before it all sinks in."

"But I am not in denial. I know perfectly well what happened, but it seems too ridiculous to believe. I am in disbelief. That's different from denial."

"I see," she said. A jewel. Not mocking me, just playing along.

"Are most people scared?"

"Yes."

"I don't feel scared. I don't seem scared to you, do I?"

"Yes." And then, very gently: "I would be, too."

It was a private room, just opposite the nurses' station. Private rooms cost dearly. I would not have chosen it. And until days later, nobody told me that I was in that room because the head nurse had wanted me nearby, to keep close watch.

That first morning was busy. A number of doctors, all residents probably, came to visit. They all looked like children. I remember two especially, because I think back on them as a pair of textbook Do and Don't illustrations, the alpha and omega of the delicate art of bedside manners.

The alpha did not introduce himself. He simply entered my room and stood at the foot of the bed, grinning at me. A stethoscope hung from the pocket of his white coat. In the beginning, many of them do this, keep the stethoscopes hanging ostentatiously out of pockets, all pockets, even out of their sports coats, even out of their overcoats, for the world to see. Later, they get over it.

This child kept grinning at me. A curious grin, half abashed, half challenging. He scratched his head. He seemed to be considering options. Finally, he spoke. "You have no idea how lucky you are," he said.

"Oh?"

"That left anterior artery of yours, the one that occluded—you know what we call that one?"

"What?"

"We call it the Widow Maker."

Had he really said that? "What did you say?"

"The *Widow Maker*. That's what we call it." Still grinning, he let it ride for a beat. Then: "You are a *very lucky lady*."

It left me breathless. Was he simply clumsy, or outright stupid? Years earlier, I had been assigned to do an article on truth-telling in medicine. It had been a hot subject then. We were in the brave new world of informed consent and patients' bills of rights, and doctors accustomed to deciding for themselves what to tell their patients—and what to withhold, and when to withhold it—now had to level with them. It was not easy to give up all that omnipotence. In a great rush of overcompensation, some of them did it in dreadfully ham-handed ways, perhaps even, some few, with a dollop of sadistic resentment mixed into the brew. I had seen one doctor walk into a patient's room and say, "Well, we just got the results back. It's cancer," and walk out.

I wondered what else might come out of the mouth of this young man at the foot of my bed, and to whom? *With your kind of brain tumor, we see them die on the table. You are a* very lucky *man. . . . Almost nobody lives past a year with this much lung disease. You are a* very lucky *woman. . . . You know what we call men with prostates like yours? We call them goners. You are a* very lucky. . . My guess was that he meant no mischief; he was just a clumsy show-off, and not the smartest kid in the class. But clumsy show-offs can do great damage.

I wanted to say something, but didn't know what. Finally, I said, "That may be more information than I need to have."

He reddened and left the room.

His opposite number was seemingly too young to shave, but he had it all together. He knocked, although the door to my room was wide open. He shook my hand. He asked if he might sit down. He asked if I were comfortable, if I had everything I needed, if I had any complaints. (Of course I did: the food, which was abysmal. I saw no reason to mention it—they all knew it—but how nice, I thought, that he thought to ask.) He said that he wanted to talk to me about my heart and proceeded to do so with the psychological astuteness of a wise old hand.

My heart muscle had been *stunned*, he said, making an emphatic little jab into the air with his fist, as though to stop the flow of air with his fist, and as a result, it could not exert enough pressure to push out blood at the optimal rate. But this was not worrisome. There was still enough pressure to do the necessary. Also, the heart's condition might improve. It might come back to normal, or closer to normal, in the following weeks, or even months. That sometimes happened. He would not be at all surprised, he said, if that happened to me. "The stent, meanwhile, will become a part of your body."

"Will I feel it?"

"Not at all. The stent will make itself at home."

That pleased me. It sounded cozy. I had a vision of this foreigner, this immigrant, coming to my shores, and my body, in its benevolence, welcoming the stranger in, inviting the stranger to make itself at home.

"And you should be encouraged by the fact that you feel so well. That is a very good sign."

Was I allowed to walk?

Sure, the resident said. It would be good for me.

I was surprised, for Hal had been bedridden for many long days after his first coronary. It had been customary then, or so I had assumed. Of course, everyone understood that many conditions were treated differently nowadays. Sick people were hauled out of bed sooner, instructed to exercise sooner, sent home much sooner, and some of it was due to the dismal economic realities—women who had just given birth, women who had just had hysterectomies; men who had just undergone various major surgeries, kicked out of the hospital sometimes overnight. But surely there were therapeutic reasons, too. Surely research had shown that it was better for patients to be moved along faster.

"Well, if I can walk, I will *walk*," I said.

"Don't overdo it," the nifty young resident said and left me his card (in case I had further questions, I was *not to hesitate* to call), and he was on his way.

I never saw him again. I'm still grateful for him.

Lunch was dreadful, as hospital food generally is, unless you are in one of those luxe country-club units that now grace many big-city hospitals, where the food is not only good but is also served by uniformed waiters. "Lunch was something they called *fish*," I reported by telephone to Al, and he arrived in midafternoon bearing fresh turkey sandwiches.

"You're doing *really* well," he said. "When I walked in yesterday, you remember how you greeted me? You said, 'Hi, cookie.'"

"I did?" Feeling pleased with myself.

"You did. You were fine, you were joking, you were *jaunty*. . . . I just couldn't believe it."

He was elated. He had telephoned my doctor. "Stuart said you'll be able to go home over the weekend. I never thought I'd get you home so soon."

Over the weekend! It was now Thursday. This was thrilling news. It seemed to reduce the fact of a heart attack to a kind of semi-nonevent.

Both of us feeling in high spirits, we set out for a walk. My husband looped his arm through mine. And it was precisely then, as he made that gesture, that everything turned surreal. Everything was powered by the most vivid sense of having been there before.

But, of course, I *had* been here before, but with roles reversed. In just that way, as Al was walking with me now, holding my arm and guiding me along, in just that way I walked with Hal, holding his arm and guiding him along, in that same hospital, in those same corridors, in the same cardiac unit, and with the same primary physician treating the same traitorous body part. I kept tripping into Hal's coronary and he into mine, even as I walked there with Al, oh, it was all so weird, and I knew that I was conflating the two men, both beloved, apart from my father the only men I had ever truly loved, confusing them now in that strange and discomforting way, joining myself now with the one and then with the other, and their own images floating into and out of each other. *I've got to straighten this out,* I thought, *or my past, the whole great tsunami of memories, will rise up and drown out my present.*

We were en route back to my room, walking by the nurses'

station when he released my arm and instead grabbed my hand and began to swing our two hands together, back and forth. As though on some signal, this made it okay. This brought me fully back to us.

This was how we had walked on West Eighty-Sixth Street one summer evening soon after we had met, strolling along hand in hand, near strangers to each other, yet knowing already that this was going to be serious.

"If anyone had told me," he had said then, "that I would be walking down the street with a woman I had recently met, swinging hands like this, I would have said that they were crazy." Because it was a scant year since Judy had died, his partner in a marriage as cherished as my own first marriage had been, and he had been immersed in sorrow and apathy and was astonished to find himself back in the world of men and women and stirrings of desire.

I reminded him now of that walk on West Eighty-Sixth Street. "Oh, *yes*," he said, and grinned. He has a marvelous grin. His face is long and slender, sharply etched, with a high forehead sloping beneath what once had been thick dark hair, sparse gray now, and near-black eyes and a neatly trimmed little salt-and-pepper Vandyke beard. A face that in repose looks contemplative, rather solemn, almost ascetic. And he is tall and very slim—("He made me think of El Greco," a friend said when she was introduced to him, catching him in one of those contemplative moments)— but when that grin breaks wide, with the lustrous teeth and the big bawdy laugh, it is contagious. Laughing now, he made me laugh too, and I thought, as I often did and still do, of our very first encounter, when he had made me cry.

chapter six

It was a dinner at the home of friends: Walter, a screen-writer, and Gloria, my literary agent—both among my near and dear.

I knew that they had invited another couple, which would make a party of five. The table was set for six. Who else was coming?

"Al Ruben, a friend of mine from the Writers Guild," Walter said. "Lovely guy. His wife died last year and he's been a basket case ever since. We've been trying to bring him out of himself." (It was the simple truth, he told me months later. There had not been the remotest thought of pairing me up with this man.)

The other couple came, drinks were served, and we were on the second round and having a merry time when the sixth guest arrived.

He did not appear to be a basket case. He appeared to be a very attractive and very cool cookie. Reserved, centered, casually dressed but buttoned up in manner. He didn't say much. He listened hard, his near-black eyes fixed like lasers.

At dinner, someone asked how long ago his wife had died. The cool cookie crumbled. Ten months ago, he said, and there was a tremor in his voice. He tried to hang onto the reserve, I could see him trying, but his face had become such a map of private places that everyone looked away. Silence descended. And in the depths of that silence, I lost it.

Suddenly, I was flailing backward through the years to when I myself had been ten months widowed, to precisely how it had felt to be ten months widowed, and oh, Jesus, it had felt so dreadful, and I began to cry. It had never happened before, but it happened this time in 3-D, a spasm of self-indulgence, crying not decorously but in the full-bodied, blubbering, nose-running way that would ruin anyone's appetite at any dinner table, and I mumbled my apologies and fled into another room to get my coat.

He came after me. It seemed extraordinary to me at the time, and still does, that this man who was still in mourning should come to comfort someone else. He took my coat, sat me down, handed me a handkerchief as I blubbered on. He kept nodding and saying, "I know, I know," and, of course, that was the thing of it: he did know. We both knew that we both knew. Mourners understand mourners, a fact that cuts handily through the minuets of Getting to Know You, and saves, as it would turn out, a great deal of time.

I finally managed to stop bawling and left, feeling wrecked; feeling furious at myself for ruining an evening that my hosts had taken the trouble to arrange. They all embraced me, except the basket case, who took my hand and said, very quietly, into my ear: "We'll see each other again."

He called ten days later, sounding awkward. "I hadn't made that kind of call in forty years," he told me much later. "I kept putting it off. I felt nervous. What would I say if I asked you out to dinner and you said no?"

Said no? I had spent the whole bloody ten days waiting and willing him to call.

In the following weeks, we saw each other often. From the very first evening, it was a take. I learned that he had grown up in Southern California, surfing off the Santa Monica beaches; that he had graduated from Columbia University; that he never wore neckties. I learned that he was a tennis nut and a bicyclist, pedaling along through Manhattan's crazed, traffic-clogged canyons with his helmet and his neat little Vandyke beard. I learned that he was an ardent lefty; that he had spent a year after college living gloriously hand to mouth in Paris and bopping around much of Europe on a motorcycle; that he had lived then for five years in London, working for a news service; that for most of his working life he had written screenplays and television scripts (*Kojak, The Defenders, Have Gun Will Travel*—all those golden oldies); and that he was now working on a screenplay about Harry Bridges, the great union organizer of the 1940s. I learned that he showed up on time and did what he said he would do and was generally, unlike me, well organized and self-disciplined. I learned that he did not enjoy cocktail-party chatter, although—or perhaps because—he adored language, and that he did enjoy small dinner parties. (Six, he said, was the ideal number.) I learned that he had a daughter, a son, a daughter-in-law, two little granddaughters. I learned that I was hooked.

One weekend, I was going to visit friends in Little Compton, Rhode Island, and he suggested that I stop by his summer house, on the Connecticut shore, on my way back to New York.

"Plan to stay overnight," he said.

"I will not stay overnight," I told Barbara in Little Compton. "That's totally out of the question."

"Why?"

"Because. I'll tell him I have to be back in New York. If I stayed overnight, there would be sex. There will *definitely* be no sex."

"Why not?"

"It's too soon." Strategic as a loopy sixteen-year-old. "It confuses the issue. I don't want him to think I just fall into bed."

I arrived at the Connecticut house. There was a long, curving, private drive, past a tennis court, beneath an allée of huge ancient trees, and I was gearing up for the sight of some dandy country mansion. But no such thing. It was a pretty little shingled Colonial, geranium boxes on the windowsills, an expansive deck overlooking a lake where a canoe and a kayak sat at the ready out back.

The master of the house was wandering around the grounds with a tool kit, inspecting loose deck boards. He moved with easy loping strides, faintly pigeon-toed, like a football player. He was bare-chested, wearing denim cutoffs over his high round butt, a red bandanna hanging out of the back pocket. He was adorable.

"Where's your overnight bag?" he asked.

I don't have an overnight bag. I can't stay. I want you to understand that I am not that kind of girl.

"It's on the back seat," I said.

It was about that time that we were strolling on West Eighty-Sixth Street, holding hands, and he said, "If anyone had told me that I would be walking down the street with a woman I had recently met, swinging hands like this, I would have said that they were crazy."

It was a surprise for me, too. In the first year after Hal's death, I myself had been something of a basket case. There may indeed be people who are ennobled by suffering, but I was not one of them. I was a perambulation of rage—rage at the fates, at the cards, the moon, the tides, rage especially at the healthy men striding past me each morning on the street, in their suits, with their briefcases, with their ruddy faces, taking up square feet of space that should have belonged to my husband. Then, slowly, the anger had burned itself out and I came back into the world. Over the years, there had been romantic attachments with men—good men, well worth loving, but never, as it happened, any I did love or wanted to live with, and I had long assumed that the way my life was going was the way it would remain, contentedly busy with work and with friends, maybe—hopefully—the occasional romance, but essentially unattached. Which was fine. I had been good at marriage. I was also good at living alone.

Then you turn a corner and bump into wild improbabilities. And to my own astonishment, there it was: myself, by now almost two decades widowed, recently ordained as a senior citizen, Medicare card in my pocket and heart on my sleeve, utterly besotted.

You would not say that we acted with the impetuosity of youth. It was months before he told his family that he was "seeing someone." ("My grandpa has a girlfriend," his five-year-old granddaughter told the neighbors.) It was a full year before he said, "Why aren't we living together?"

I was both thrilled and wary, being so accustomed to my

own way of living and doing. But the thrilled won over the wary. We consolidated households. My own apartment, a Fifth Avenue penthouse overlooking Central Park—which Hal and I had bought back in the days when you didn't have to be rich to buy a Fifth Avenue penthouse overlooking Central Park—was a gem, but too small for two writers who each needed a home office. I moved into Al's home, a sprawling apartment in a venerable building facing Central Park on the Upper West Side, where he and his late wife had raised their children.

Those first months were not easy. We were both out of the habit of compromise, flexible as a pair of wooden yardsticks. That's the way of it, often enough, when older couples come together—all those decades of psychic cement to crack through. We had agreed to combine household effects, but the effort to do so damn near ruined us. Whose dining chairs at whose dining table? Whose carpets on which floors? Rearranging artwork, things that we had collected and loved with our late mates, arguing about which painting should hang on what wall, or whether it should hang anywhere at all . . . We thought that we were arguing about the paintings, but, of course, it was not about *things*. Such arguments are never simply about things. It was about control.

But we learned to bend toward each other. And what helped us bend—a surprise, a sweet bonus—was the way the past began to inform the present.

There was a very long hallway in the apartment, leading from the living room to the master bedroom and lined on both walls with dozens of his family pictures, the record of several generations of shared lives—Al and Judy's parents and grandparents, Al and Judy as infants, as schoolchildren, as college graduates with mortarboards, as bride and groom, as new parents, and then as parents of the groom, and then, smiling ecstatically, cradling their grandchildren—all the usual, precious stuff.

When I first had moved in, he had asked, "Do you mind the pictures? Should I take them down?"

In fact, I loved the pictures. I loved the sense of roots made palpable. In time, that collection was joined by my own family pictures, my grandparents' wedding, my parents' wedding, my own first wedding, the bridal picture of Hal and Martha hanging near the bridal picture of Al and Judy, each somehow giving the nod to the other, and finally, moving right along on those walls, through those first years, all the inevitable Al-and-Martha pictures, our personal growth chart, and with each addition, the walls became increasingly richer, as such walls always do, in continuity. That is the juiciest stuff, continuity. It may be love that makes the world go round, but continuity is what keeps it on its axis.

If those first months were sometimes fraught, they were also great fun. The sheer novelty of *us* made it feel, in a way, like playing house. (I called him Albert back then. He didn't tell me, until years later, that he thought it was because I found *Al* too close to *Hal*. I didn't tell him, until years later, that he was right.)

Then came a morning, three months after I'd moved in, when it stopped feeling like playing house. It came with a terrible discontinuity.

I was in the kitchen having breakfast and reading *The Times*. (Reading the obits first, as I had begun to do in recent years.) Al's telephone rang. Moments later, he came into the kitchen, turned on the little television set that we kept on a counter, then stood behind me and put his hands on my shoulders.

We saw the first tower aflame. We saw the second plane slam into the second tower. We saw masses of people, looks of terror on their faces, running in a narrow street. We heard an announcer wailing again and again, "Oh my God no. Oh my God no. Oh my God no."

All morning we stood at the window watching the hordes walking uptown, in a plodding, single-file sort of way, along Central Park West. There was no crowd noise. There was no visible animation. They simply walked. We understood, much later, that they had been walking for hours, traveling up from the holocaust some six miles south, toward home, by the only means available.

In the afternoon, hearing television reports that hospital emergency teams were at the ready, awaiting injured survivors, we walked across the park toward Mount Sinai, the hospital nearest to us, to give whatever help we could. I still remember the cloudless brilliance of that sky, the utter serenity of those park paths. We emerged on the East Side and walked toward the hospital, braced for terrible sights.

There were none. The doctors and nurses stood waiting, outside the hospital, many in green scrub suits. The ambulances lined the curbs. There was no action. There were no takers. There were no survivors.

Then it no longer felt like playing house.

It seems morally reprehensible to use large human events, devastating events, to personal purpose, but we all do it. It is such a compellingly convenient way to correct our perspectives.

We could no longer get too exercised over whose painting hung where.

Four years later, we decided to seek further consolidation.

On a freezing February afternoon, icicles hanging off the rock masses in Central Park, salt strewn on the icy sidewalks, traffic in a ponderous jumble, we took the subway downtown to the New York Bureau of Licenses.

A security guard stood outside the doors, a huge fellow, gloved and mufflered and stomping against the cold. Al asked him, "Where do we go for a license?"

"What kind of license?"

"Marriage license."

"For who?"

"For us."

The guard regarded the pair of seniors who stood before him. He looked suspicious. "For . . . you?" Waving his forefinger like a metronome between the two of us.

We nodded.

"No *kidding*. You folks are getting married? Fan*tastic!*" Pulled off his cap and punched the air. Pulled off a glove, grabbed Al's hand and gave it a shake that Al thought, he said later, might have broken small bones. "Hey, Mike, come over here. Get this! These folks are getting *married*!"

Mike, too, seemed intensely pleased.

It was much the same story when we went to the jewelry district in Midtown for a wedding band. The saleswoman was clearly confused. "For . . . your daughter?" she asked.

"For us."

"For *you*? Oh, I love it. I *love* it. Helen! Stacy! Listen . . ."

It was a small family wedding. The florist, the wine merchant, the cake maker—all strangers—all expressed joy far beyond any commercial call of duty. In our first marriages, Al's and mine, we had gotten no such joyous response from strangers. We understood that it was impersonal. It was a glimpse into the realm of possibilities. The hope for renewal, the second chance, the never-too-late.

How bountiful I felt, to be spreading a little stardust.

So here we were now, seven years married. We had marked the passage of those years not so much with the wedding anniversaries as with the birthday trips. Those trips had always resonated in some especially celebratory way. I don't know why. The record of them hung on the picture walls: Al and Martha lolling on beaches, palm trees in the background, or squinting at the skyline in some great gritty city—eleven years' worth, counting the premarriage trips, of Al and Martha grinning into the camera. And now another birthday was coming up and we had planned to be celebrating in Charleston, a honey of a city, where we had gone for a previous birthday celebration.

Change of plan. We would celebrate at home instead. Home for the weekend, the doctors had told the birthday boy. Given the alternative, I was ecstatic.

The forecast was for snow. Home for a White Halloween. What a trick. What a treat.

chapter seven

An Indian summer snowstorm, as forecast. "A once-in-a-hundred-year event!" a TV weatherman said, sounding gleeful as a kid with a sled. Out my window were rare sights: trees still covered with leaves, leaves now covered with snow, hanging on for dear truncated life, beneath the weight of the October surprise.

I had been awake since dawn, planning the birthday dinner: pork roast, baked potato (dry for him—he rejects the creams and butters I love to slather on; he has the body and the cholesterol count of a skinny young stud), sautéed spinach, Julie's killer chocolate cake, all his favorites.

Change of plan.

The first hint that all was not well came with the arrival of my nurse practitioner. This is a category that didn't exist when I last spent time in hospitals. This is a nurse with advanced training, certified to do some of what doctors traditionally do, such as ordering tests and prescribing medications.

It seemed likely that Carla's advanced training had included bedside manners. She was a darling—open-faced, hands-on, exuding cheer and optimism. But when you have to tell people things they do not want to hear, there is only so much cheer and optimism you can exude. Carla solved this problem by using a strategy that a Wall Street trader I once knew had employed whenever he had to give a client bad news. He called it Making the Sandwich.

To Make the Sandwich, you begin by delivering some good news, which is the bottom slice of bread, then you lay on the bad news, which is the filling, and finally you deliver another piece of good news, which is the top slice of bread, so that you always end up on the sunny side of the message. ("You can always find *some* good news," the Wall Street man had said. "Or make it up.") I have tried it. It's a nice little strategy. Sometimes it even works.

"You seem *much* better this morning," Carla said. Happy

face. "But"—serious face—"we need to see you free of pain. Now, let's hope"—smiling again—"by tomorrow . . ."

"Pain? What pain?"

"Last night. You told your nurse last night that you were having some pain in your chest."

"Oh, that was nothing. It was just a little sore, shallow, like what you get from a bruise. That wouldn't be my heart, would it?"

"It could be. Heart attacks are so different for different people. It's not always that crushing pain, you know, the 'Hollywood Heart Attack,' especially not for women. Sometimes it's more like gastritis. You might get shortness of breath, nausea, fatigue—of course, fatigue can have so many other causes, it's not usually a symptom of a heart attack, but it *could* be—or you might even have no pain at all. I mean, it presents in so many different ways, it's crazy. But now that you know how it presents *for you*, you'll know next time."

She must have heard the words as though she were hearing them through my ears, for suddenly she looked stricken. "No, no, *no!*" she said, waving a hand vigorously in front of her face, as though swatting away flies. "I didn't mean that you'll have another heart attack. I just meant that if you ever had the same symptoms, you'd know."

"So are you telling me"—listen, I know this good news/ bad news game—"that I can't go home today?"

"We just want to keep an eye on you a little longer. . . ."

"But I *have* to go home today. It's my husband's *birthday.*" *Oh, come on. Birthday, shmirthday. What is this, a party for a five-year-old, with the cupcakes and all? What are you getting so desperate about?*

She tried gamely for another sandwich—"*Nothing* is going to happen to you." Beat. "But if anything *did* happen . . ." Beat. ". . . wouldn't you rather be here, where we can . . ."— but the thing began falling apart with that second slice of bread, and she gave it up.

"Maybe tomorrow," she said, giving an encouraging lit- tle pat to my toe that lay under the sheet before departing.

Stuart had already signed off for the weekend. The doctor who was covering for him showed up midmorning. A chic woman, in her fifties, hair done just so, expensive designer trench coat and big, luxurious leather bag, high heels clicking smartly on the vinyl tile floor as she approached my bed. And she was an exceedingly cool customer—as cool as Carla had been warm. Exceptions granted, I think it is fair to say that this is one of the primary distinctions between doctors and nurses.

"I can't discharge you today," the doctor said. No sandwich here.

"Why not?"

"We want to see your signs more stable."

"What's wrong with my signs?"

"Something happened this morning."

"What?"

"It's not clear. Something."

She seemed secretive. I didn't trust her. "I'm supposed to go home today. My doctor said that I could."

"I can't keep you from leaving, but I advise against it."

"Well, I'm not about to go counter to a doctor's orders. That would be dumb." She smiled slightly and nodded in agreement. "But I'd like to have some idea of what 'something' means."

"We're not sure yet. There was a big bump in your EKG early this morning. When you get a bump like that, it means that something is going on, but we can't be sure what."

"Another heart attack?" I was scared now.

"Well, I wouldn't say it's more . . . but something happened, okay?"

That "okay?" left me seething. Translation: Stop nagging me. But what about my informed consent? What about my patients' bill of rights? What about my right to know?

I want to know.

But maybe they really don't know.

Oh, likely story. They know all right. What they know is that knowledge is *power*, information is *power*, and so they hoard information, they dole it out reluctantly, parsimoniously, in little sticky syllabic bits, *some-thing happened* . . . because if the patient is given all the information, the patient might know enough to have *thoughts* about the course of her *treatment*, the patient might feel some modest modicum of *control* over her *body*, the patient might want to be *consulted* about her *care*, the patient might expect, God forbid, a *place* at the *table*, none of which must be allowed to happen because it would bring the whole damned elitist edifice down upon your well-coifed head, your Blahnik heels, your Burberry trench coat . . . Listen, you icicle, I pay for that trench coat! You come clickity-clacking your way in and out of here in three and a half minutes and then I get some humongous bill, of which I will pay twenty percent and Medicare will pay the rest, which means that we *all* pay the rest, we are *all* paying for that fucking trench coat, and what are we getting for the money but a great big phony-baloney "*Something happened*" . . . ?

Going on and on like that, by now in a full-blown rage. And, of course, it had nothing to do with the doctor. If there was a whiff of elitism in her manner, that was the way of the breed; I had known few doctors who did not give off a whiff of that particular essence. But she had behaved in a responsible way, refusing to discharge a patient whose vital signs were unstable, telling me truthfully, as it turned out, all that she knew, and I was simply piling my fear-fueled rage—impotent rage, which has always been the emotion that I find hardest to handle sanely—upon her altogether blameless shoulders. Rage because, for reasons unknown, I was not going home.

Impotent rage. And now my lunch tray appears. I am ready for it.

Sitting on this tray, amid such inedibles as probably grace the lunch trays in big-city hospitals across the country, is a bottle that I have never seen before. The bottle is red. It is some six inches tall, made of rigid plastic, with a big, vividly colored, wraparound label whose front panel says:

For Institutional Use Only
BOOST
Nutritional Energy Drink

A side label informs me, "Key Nutrients to Keep You Going Strong."

The back label lists the ingredients. It reads as follows:

"Ingredients: water, corn syrup solids, sugar, vegetable oil (canola, high oleic sunflower, corn oils), milk protein concentrate, calcium calceinate, sodium caseinate, and less than 0.5% of potassium citrate, magnesium chloride, soy lecithin, calcium phosphate, salt, ascorbic acid, sodium ascorbate, beta carotene, biotin, niacinamide, calciumpantothenate, vitamin B12, vitamin B6 hydrochloride, riboflavin, thiamine hydrochloride, folic acid, potassium iodine, magnesium phosphate, natural and artificial flavor, choline chloride, vitamin E acetate, vitamin A palmitate, vitamin D3, vitamin K1, carrageenan, potassium chloride, zinc sulfate, manganese sulfate, cupric sulfate, chromic chloride, sodium molybdate, sodium selenite, ferrous sulfate."

Are they kidding?

A brief questionnaire:

1. The phrase "For Institutional Use Only" usually connotes a freebie, as with those little soaps in hotel bathrooms. Was this product a freebie?
2. If so, was there a quid pro quo?
3. If so, what was the quid pro quo?
4. Who authorized the distribution of this product to patients in this hospital?
5. Why?

*   *   *

By the time Al called, I was primed for a fight.

"Water, corn syrup solids, sugar—for openers. Can you believe it?" I said.

"Never mind that. Tell me what the doctor said."

"I told you. I can't go home. Some birthday."

"And that's all she told you, that something happened, and she wouldn't tell you any more than that?"

"She said they don't know. She said, 'Something happened, okay?' but they don't know what. Like hell they don't know what."

"Maybe they don't, Martha."

"Like hell."

"Well, look. We'll celebrate there."

"When? Tonight?"

"No, I'll come over this afternoon."

"Why aren't you coming over for dinner?" Peevish, hating the sound of my own voice.

"To tell you the truth, I'd rather not have to eat dinner there. It's just not comfortable to eat there."

Not comfortable? Does he suppose, then, that I am lolling here in a feather bed? Damn! He is not supposed to say that. He is supposed to say, *Of course* I'll come over tonight. *Of course* I'll have dinner with you. I wouldn't *dream* of not having dinner with you.

Not comfortable? On a dime, I hate him. "I don't want to talk anymore now," I say, and hang up, and cry.

An aide comes into the room. "What's the matter?" she asks.

What's the matter is that I am facing mortality alone.

Hal wouldn't ever have let me face mortality alone. Hal would have been here. Hal would have eaten dinner here. Hal would have eaten every meal here. Hal would have *slept* here, for chrissake. Hal was a saint.

Of course. I have learned this in my wanderings among the solo acts: all ex-wives are crazy, all ex-husbands are bastards, and all dead spouses are saints. It is remarkable, really, how consistently this is so.

I did once hear a woman who had just buried her husband say, "He was always a selfish son of a bitch and I'm not going to say anything different just because he's dead." But she was an exception.

Something happened, okay?

Now every little twitch became a threat. Here, at this very moment, this sensation. Right down here, deep, between my breasts. Just . . . *something*, nothing much, but not *nothing*, less than a pain, more than a slight ache, what the hell should I call it? What are the protocols? Where are the borders? Where are the boundaries? When does a twinge become an ache become a pain become a cry for help?

Twice that afternoon, after the chic doctor's visit, I reported what I called "a little something."

"What do you mean, 'a little something'? Pain?"

"No, not really pain. Just sort of . . . something there. A feeling. Kind of a heaviness. An ache."

Twice they came running with the EKG cart, because they do not fool around with someone who had a heart attack seventy-two hours ago.

And twice there was nothing.

I was embarrassed. I said as much to Lianne, one of the aides, a huge, gentle woman who could embrace you in a bear hug without ever touching. She said, "Honey, don't you be embarrassed. It's *your heart*." The aide Sam, who was tidying my bed linens, and who smiled all the time, as though he had things to be happy about—although Lianne had told me that he had an overfull plate, with various harsh troubles at home—patted my shoulder and said, "*Your heart*, baby."

But after the second EKG, one of the residents came

by and gave me a gentle scolding. "The next time you feel *something*," he said, "would you please ask the nurse for a Maalox, and then wait half an hour to see if the feeling goes away?"

Fair enough. Every time I feel *something* and someone comes rushing with that EKG cart and someone else has to attach those suction cups and a third someone then has to read that printout, I am squandering the time and effort of people who are overworked and understaffed, not to speak of the expense of the test itself, which must be considerable, since there appears to be no such thing as a cheap medical test, which means that the expense must get passed on to other patients in one form or another, which means that my *little something* is costing *everyone* money, just like that Burberry trench coat.

Oh, Christ, I thought, I so deeply do not want to become a cardiac kvetch. It happens so easily. Fresh-minted cardiacs are such a nervous breed, always looking for trouble.

I remember writing, quoting Hal, "For someone who has had a heart attack, there is no such thing as a casual pain in the chest." How precisely on the money, something I couldn't have known back then.

I remember hearing from one of his cardiologists about patients who have cardiac phobias. A cardiac phobia? What is *that*? I asked, reportorially intrigued by the phrase, and the doctor said, "Oh, that's actually pretty common. We have patients who come in here regularly with chest pain, convinced they're having heart attacks. Very often it's guys whose fathers died of heart attacks, and every year, a couple of weeks before the anniversary of the death, they'll start having those pains and they'll come in here terrified that they're dying, and there's never anything wrong with them."

Imagine, I had thought at the time. Imagine the blessing of that: crying a bucket, with nothing to cry about. As opposed to those who have plenty to cry about, and never do cry.

I remember Hal's fingers in constant play across his chest, testing the inner weather, the fingers betraying the anxiety he never expressed aloud.

I remember a nurse in the men's cardiac care unit telling me that you could always tell the sky-high level of anxiety by the sky-high level of masturbation.

That is not an appealing idea, easing my anxiety with masturbation. But I do dearly wish that I could ease it with a gin martini.

Okay. I am fearful and I am expressing it around the block. What I need is to learn how to manage my fear. I wish I could discuss this with Hal. We used to have such helpful posthumous discussions. Nothing mystical in this. I have no talent for mystical things. It is simply that, for some time after he died, I had the sense that he was still with me, or, rather, *within* me, dissolved and flowing within me like some natural substance, like blood. (Actually this is a common sensation among mourners—*internalizing*, the psychotherapists call it—and very nice. More comforting than Valium or booze, although, I must say, they came in handy, too.)

Whenever I had this sensation—which, regrettably, was sustained for only moments at a time—I would feel not diminished by his death but bigger, stronger, wiser than before, being then not merely myself but the sum of all that we had been together; and I could use his common sense, of which he had always had plenty more than I, as though it were my own. So that I could, for example, say to him, "Listen, today the loss of you hurts too much to bear. What should I do?"

And this voice that flowed within me would say: "What you need is distraction. Pull up your socks and go see a movie."

"I don't want to go see a movie." We are so loyal to our miseries.

"Force yourself."

Which I would do. And though I sat through many clunkers, his advice proved as solid in death as it had been in life. I always felt better after the show.

From this, I learned a valuable lesson about distraction, a strategy that usually gets a bad rap.

It was the great sage Frank Sinatra who said, or was said to have said, that he was in favor of anything that helps you get through the night. Psychotherapists, by and large, do not agree. Psychotherapists like to say that when you are dealing with loss—any kind, of a loved one, of a marriage, of a job, of a healthy heart—you must *experience the grief* (*do the work of bereavement* is another popular phrase), rather than trying to escape from it.

This may be wise, or it may be just a thing to say and next year they will say something else. That happens a lot in the behavioral sciences. But the lesson I learned the hard way, and which I pass on here with provisional guarantees, is that when the choice is between distraction and *experiencing the grief,* go for the distraction every time. If it works, you're ahead of the game. If not, you're no worse off than before.

This helpful posthumous dialogue, in which I had not engaged in three decades and which I now lay in a hospital bed struggling to summon up again, had begun in the most unspectacular way.

It had been just a few weeks since Hal's death. I had spent those weeks in a trance of grief and semidisbelief, fueled by anger at this dearly beloved one who had dared to desert me by dying. I was drinking and pill-popping my way through mostly sleepless nights. I was bloated with self-pity. I was a mess.

Condolence callers were still arriving daily. There had been food enough to feed an army, and now there was not. Marketing needed to be done. But for one brief trip to the local liquor store, in the course of which I had looked angrily away from all those healthy men coming toward me, with their strong strides, I hadn't been out of the house since the memorial service. But now I roused myself—a considerable act of will—and decided to go to the noted market Zabar's, where a raging spirit might be soothed by the perfumes of the delicatessen counter.

I took the Ninety-Sixth Street crosstown bus, then began walking downtown along Broadway. I could not comprehend the normalcy of it. The world looked as it always had. There they all were, the usual ancients bent low by their widows' humps and their walkers, the usual weirdos shouting deprecations at no one in particular, the usual

users nodding on the benches, everyone looking as everyone always did, normal, or normally abnormal, remarkably
unaware, unaffected, unimpressed, indifferent to the recent
occurrence of a cosmic event. I resented this, but there was
nothing to be done.

At the Zabar's bread counter, which was as always a zoo,
I put in my order for bagels and rye and waited. A voice
behind me said, "Martha, did you ever try the seven-grain
bread? It's delicious."

I turned and knew that I knew her, but couldn't think
of how.

"Carrie Bender," she said. "We met at the Wallaces'."

"Of course. Hello."

"I heard about your loss. Such a lovely man, your husband. I can't tell you how sorry I am."

"Thank you."

"I know what you're going through. I lost my husband, too."

"I'm so sorry."

"We should talk."

"Yes."

"Why don't we go have coffee?"

"Now? Oh, but I have to . . ." I don't want to go have
coffee. No offense, but I do not want to join your Widows'

Coffee Club, you do not know what I am going through, because your loss is yours and my loss is mine and never the twain . . .

Oh, stop it, Martha. Ungenerous bitch. Remember Hal saying, "Almost everyone almost always means well." Here is a woman who means well. She has been, as she says, through it. Perhaps she can help you with this *work of bereavement*, and you surely can use whatever help you can get.

How long had she been widowed, I asked as we sat over coffee. I had grown voracious for numbers, I wanted quantifiable answers from the less recently bereaved. *How long was it before you started feeling better? How much better? How many months before you could sleep through the night?* And so forth.

Her husband had died four years earlier, she said.

And how had she gotten through that first year?

She had spent it in bed.

"In bed?"

"Yes, mostly. I was so depressed I could hardly get up. I never left the house. I never got dressed."

"Never got dressed?"

"I spent the whole first year in his bathrobe. I would just put on his bathrobe and lie around the house all day. All day," she said firmly, as though giving me a cooking instruction: marinate the meat all day.

I understood about the bathrobe. I was already making heavy use of the bathrobe. But never getting dressed? Never leaving the house?

"When did you start getting over it?" I asked.

"You never get over it. You'll see."

Silence and dread. I sat staring into my cheese Danish, trying to parse this in a reasonable way. To say that you never get over it might mean simply that you never forget, which was fair enough, even desirable. If you had loved, why would you ever want to forget? My father—besides Hal, the only other man I had ever adored—had been dead for fifteen years then, and at first the pain had seemed too much to bear. But it had long since evolved into a nostalgia that became not only bearable, but also precious, the legacy of a love that had illuminated my childhood.

But what I heard this poor woman saying was that her pain had never evolved into nostalgia, or into anything else at all—it had remained unalloyed pain. Was this in the cards for me?

And then it hit me. I said, "Tell me, were you given to depression before your husband died?"

"Oh, *yes*," she said.

I went home and relived the meeting aloud, as though describing it to Hal. I had never done such a thing before and I don't know why I did it then, but that was what I did. And that was when that inner voice began to flow within me, and spoke its first words, which I recognized instantly as the start of an ongoing conversation.

"I don't want to end up living in your bathrobe," I said.

"Then choose not to," the voice said. Which remains, to this day, the best advice anyone has ever given me about anything.

Of course, these posthumous talks were possible only because I did not grasp that my husband was dead. Not really; not on that plane of reality on which we live most of our emotional lives. I grasped that he *had died*, but not that he was *dead*. There are crucial distinctions. A plane crash, a shooting or knifing, a sudden chest-clenching collapse upon a sunny suburban tennis court, or even if it happens in some long, slow way, there is always that very moment of departure, that precise micromoment when everything stops, and doctors don't know why really. This mystery taunts them, medical students are forever asking, and the doctors cannot answer, why at that very pinpoint in time, all systems close down and out, so that however it happens, a being is one instant there and the next instant nowhere, nothing, nonexistent, nevermore. Who can grasp such things? Not I. They are mere facts. Facts are easy to grasp objectively. Subjectively, *ah*. Subjectively is a whole other story.

The subjective is an elusive plane of reality. It takes time to get there. Almost nobody gets there right away, which is why new mourners so typically feel "numb." Some people get there quickly—a few weeks, a month or two, perhaps. But I was a slow study. It took me almost a year.

Then came a fine spring morning when I was driving home to Manhattan from a weekend in the country. Six-lane highway, traffic brisk, sun shining, Beethoven blaring, feeling, actually, pretty *good*, rolling along at seventy in the fast lane, and making a progress report to the dear departed.

"So last night I went to a dinner party," I was saying, "and I didn't think of you once. Are you pleased?"

"I am," that inner voice said.

"And I was seated beside a man who asked if he could call me. He said he'd like to take me out to dinner. What do you think?"

"What does it matter what I think?"

"I need to know."

"Did you like him?"

"He wasn't you."

"Did you like him?"

"He's a widower."

"Did you like him?"

"He seemed nice."

"Then go to dinner."

"But a *date*. For heaven's sake, Hal. It isn't even a year yet. It makes me feel guilty."

"It does not make you feel guilty. You choose to feel guilty."

I was about to concede the point when there came a frightening explosive sound, a sound like a rifle shot hard by my ear, and the car went out of control. It took off like a wild animal, careening across the lanes, while I turned the wheel frantically in the opposite direction and hit the brake hard—exactly the wrong thing to do in a blowout, but what did I know of blowouts? I was going on dumb instinct—and then the car began to make circles, spinning around and around and around, then slowing down almost to a halt, and I looked up and saw that I was in the center lane facing the wrong way, cars speeding directly toward me, horrified faces floating behind windshields, intimations of screams vibrating in the air, and I thought,

Echoes of Heartsounds

Well, now, here we go, good-bye world, hello Hal, for death was certain, no escape, and I sat peering into the abyss and waiting for the hit, but instead, those cars went parting around me like the waters of the biblical sea, they swerved stage right onto the shoulder and stage left into the fast lane, it should have been a front-page disaster but it was not, just, I am sure, a good many badly shaken souls, and then traffic gave way so that my car and I were able to limp up onto the center island, where we both finally collapsed and I slumped there, disbelieving, pinching my arms, trying to absorb the impossible fact—here we are again, with those objective and subjective realities—that I was still alive.

I opened the door to get out, but when I tried to stand, my legs were trembling too hard to hold me and I fell to the ground and lay crying, soaking the sweet fresh grass, the sun still shining, the Beethoven still blaring. At one point, I looked out to the road and saw the traffic passing very slowly, the rubberneckers staring with that avid, almost buoyant curiosity, but nobody stopped, not a soul ever stopped, and I wept on, admiring the dimensions of my grief and my drama and my redemption.

Then I had a thought. It was very clear. I thought (this being years before cell phones), I must get to a telephone right away. I must call Hal and tell him, "Listen, I was almost killed on the Long Island Expressway, but I am all right and not to worry and I will be home soon."

But wait. Some problem here. What is it, what is it?

Oh, yes. I can't call Hal. Hal is dead.

Whom, then, am I to call?

And had, in that instant, the most piercing sense that this was what marriage meant: Marriage meant that there was someone in the world whom you must call—not those whom you *may* call, not the relatives and friends who hold you dear and who would grieve if you were gone, but the one person, even if, let's say, you do not hold each other so dear, the one person whom it would be unthinkable *not* to call—a matter of basic domestic civility, like calling to say that you won't be home for dinner—and to whom you say, "Listen, I was almost killed on the Long Island Expressway but I am all right and not to worry and I will be home soon."

Weeping heroically now, really getting into it, total sensory immersion, powerful thoracic contractions, neuroelectric convulsions, transports of adrenal flooding, the whole soaring business, I congratulated myself upon this insight. Yes, this was what marriage meant, and this was what I no longer had, and this was the precise moment in which I became, not simply in my legal papers but in the official-dom of my blood, a widow.

And after that, I spoke to Hal no more.

So here I was now, almost three decades later, afraid of my treacherous heart and needing urgently to find relief from my fear.

Hal, I said to the ceiling, I am driving these good people crazy with my 'little somethings' and I need distraction. I need your advice.

No answer.

I kept trying for a long while, concentrating hard, as I suppose believers do at a séance, but nothing happened. It is awkward to get a conversation going after decades of silence.

Very well, I thought, I will have to work it out for myself.

A private conversation:

Martha, why do your hands shake?

I am fearful.

Of what?

Of another heart attack.

Why fearful?

Because something happened.

What?

I don't know.

Right. You don't know. Are there any signs, symptoms, auras, omens, of another heart attack?

Oh, yes. All the above.

Such as?

This thing that I feel at the moment. This presence, as we say, when we do not know what else to call it, right here, this slightly ominous rather heavy presence down at my sternum, this pale reminder of what I felt when I had my first (the next time, Carla said, I would know*) myocardial infarction.*

It could be gastritis.

Exactly my point. Gastritis can mean a heart attack.

Alternatively, gastritis can mean gastritis.

So I should ask for the Maalox?

Good idea. You know, we can feel symptoms in any body part if we concentrate hard enough. Here is my right arm. It feels perfectly fine. But if I concentrate hard on this arm, soon I will feel a pulse throbbing, a joint aching, the blood coursing . . . Is it possible you are thinking too hard?

Very possible. This is the classic response to a first MI. We think too hard, we concentrate too fiercely, we are exquisitely sensitive to every little incipience of a sensation of presence here in the vicinity of the heart, we are forever struggling to find the demarcations between the worrisome and the benign, and this inconvenient overabundance of concentration goes on, they say, until the neophyte cardiac becomes desensitized. . . .

And how long does that take?

How the fuck should I know?

Al came with sandwiches, and ate off a paper plate resting on the arm of the aqua-colored Naugahyde visitors' chair. Then we took a long walk down several long corridors, swinging arms together in that old way, and when he left I kissed him and told him Happy Birthday and loved him very much.

I said, "I'm just so sorry I can't be home today."

He said, "So you'll be home tomorrow. How much difference does a day make?"

chapter eight

I was submerged in a vat of ice. I was drowning. I tried to escape, tried to curl off to the side and into a ball, but I couldn't seem to move easily, and the ice was everywhere. I cried out "Help!" and when no one appeared, I cried out again, and finally somebody came.

"You said, 'Am I dead yet?'" the head nurse Noreen told me later. "You were shaking violently. It was 73 degrees in here. You kept begging for your sweater. We couldn't find your sweater. We piled blankets on you, and you still kept crying you were cold."

"What was happening?"

"Chills and spiking fever."

"From what?"

"You got an infection."

"How?"

She shrugged. "Probably from the IV. Or from . . . there's just no way to know."

"When was that? How long have I been here?"

"You were brought here from the CCU last Friday. You had the chills and fever on Monday, Halloween night. Today is Wednesday. When you came here, they wanted to put you in a double room down the hall. I said no. I said, 'She has to be in this single room right near the nurses' station, so we can watch her. She seems stable, but there could be complications.' Then you remember that big snowstorm the day before Halloween? And then, the very next night, you started spiking. So that infection was already brewing, and it was a good thing we had you in this room opposite us."

Infection. The same old hospital bugaboo. Only once before had I ever been hospitalized, for removal of a benign tumor. It should have been no big deal, but that time, too, I had become infected and ended up with acute peritonitis, which had turned into a very big deal indeed.

They hadn't had hand-sanitizing dispensers in every hospital room then, but they do now, and there probably hasn't been this much talk about the importance of washing hands since the 1850s, when the hapless Hungarian doctor Ignaz Semmelweis was pleading with his colleagues to wash their hands before attending women in childbirth, who were dying at awful rates of infection (then called "childbed fever"). This was decades before there was any notion of a germ theory. Semmelweis was flying blind, somehow sensing what must be done, and was cruelly ridiculed and ostracized for his trouble. He became mentally ill, was institutionalized, was beaten by guards when he resisted them, and died, at age forty-seven, of—cue the irony—infection, probably brought on by the beatings.

A hundred and fifty years after poor heroic Semmelweis, the problem persists. Hospitals do their best, and it did look to me as though the medical staffers were forever pumping stuff out of that dispenser fixed to the wall by my door, but hospital-acquired infection (HAI) still causes, or contributes to, some one hundred thousand deaths a year in American hospitals, despite all efforts to prevent it.

In the morning, the fever and chills were gone, but what had developed overnight was a new complication. Phlebitis.

A beauty of a bump, roughly the size of a halved golf ball, was perched on the inside of my left arm, midway between the shoulder and the crook of the arm. It was a bizarre sight, a new topographic feature in the landscape of me that had arisen suddenly, out of the plain, overnight.

A vein in the crook now bulged forth, hard and angry-looking, like the cord in a very old neck. Shoulder to elbow, the arm weighed a thousand pounds and throbbed with pain.

All day, doctors came and went. Blood was taken several times. I hate having my blood taken. My veins are tiny, the only petite part of me, and nurses often have trouble getting into them and make bad hits, which makes the nurses anxious and less likely to make good hits. One tried his damnedest but missed on three tries, each time causing more pain in the infected arm. By the time he quit trying, we were both near tears, he apologizing for his misses, I apologizing for my veins, and another nurse finished the job.

There was talk of calling in the infectious diseases people. There was talk of antibiotic treatments. What there was no talk of, a subject lost deep in the mists, was the subject of going home.

They took me downstairs for an echocardiogram. The gurneys were lined up two by two, waiting to enter their various arks. It was cold, and an aide was dispensing heated blankets, which felt heavenly. On the gurney beside me lay a very old man, at least ninety. Motionless, eyes closed, face skeletal, like an Auschwitz face. He looked comatose. But when the aide approached him with the blankets, his head reared up suddenly and he cried out, in a loud, commanding wail, "*Mommy! Mommy!*"

I shivered.

Al and I sat gazing at each other glumly in the early-evening light. The nighttime nurse came on.

"Well, what's happened to you?" she said.

Al answered. "A blood infection. Iatrogenic."

"What's that?"

I, testily: "You don't know that word? It means 'caused in the hospital.' How long have you been a nurse?"

She, frostily: "Two years. And the reason I don't know that word is that we never used it in training. It was called 'nosocomial.'"

Al checked it out. She was right. Nosocomial: originating in the hospital. Iatrogenic: caused by medical treatment.

I apologized to her.

Dr. Hearst, head of the infectious diseases department and an eminence in his field, came to confer with me. He sat on the edge of the bed, which I liked, and spoke in a straightforward way—a dialogue of colleagues, which was the welcome illusion—of the rich variety of staphylococcal infections. They can be bad or not so bad, he said. This one that appeared to have infected me—a *Staph aureus* infection of the bloodstream, with mortality rates (he didn't tell me this part; I looked it up later) ranging from 20 to 40 percent, and over 80 percent if left untreated—this one was a very bad bug.

How would it be treated?

That wasn't certain yet. Probably they would recommend a concentrated course of antibiotics, administered intravenously.

For how long? Five days, as with those packets of antibiotic pills?

Four weeks.

Oh God.

Well, he said, there were three alternatives: if we went with that course of treatment, it could be done here in the hospital, or in a nursing home, or I could be treated in my own home, by a licensed nurse.

Treatment at home? Yes! What could be better?

Whereupon my colleague, sitting there at the edge of the bed, filled in the picture. Treatment at home would be expensive: $500 a day just for the antibiotic, in addition to the substantial cost for the nurse, who would have to come three times a day, seven days a week, to administer the IV, and none of it was covered by Medicare. Add to this the downside of not being in hospital if I got into any kind of trouble.

The nursing-home alternative, I rejected outright. Those were the places you never left, except in a box. Coursing in my blood was the memory of a beloved grandmother who had lived with us, with my parents and my brother and me, from the time she was widowed (how bittersweet, to remember that this used to be the norm; when did it become the exception, and why?); and who, upon the advice of the family doctor, had been moved to a nursing home to recover from some ailment, and she had recovered and recovered and recovered there until she died there, the question of her discharge somehow lost in a tangle of red tape and medical advice. My mother, to her own dying day, had never forgiven herself for letting her mother die in that place.

And recently there had been the case of a friend, a brilliant man beset by a slew of ailments, who had gone to one of those places for the same reason: to recover. I had visited him there, seen the elders slumped catatonic in their wheelchairs lining the corridor walls, seen him sitting among them, head in his hands, staring into some grim personal space, smelled that odor—that characteristic ineffable odor of such places, attar of dust, decay, urine, grief, fear, hopelessness, eruptions of gas, exhalations of bile, floor wax, room fresheners (carnation, lavender, lily-of-the-valley), ammonia cleaners, astringent sanitizers—and I had thought, Oh, sweet Jesus, if sickness isn't enough to finish a body off, this place could do it.

So no. No nursing home.

Then there was the third alternative—stay in the hospital, which the staff encouraged me to do.

Al wanted me home. "Let's sleep on it," he said, which is what you always say about the indecisions that will keep you sleepless.

Soon after Dr. Hearst left, Carla, the Making-the-Sandwich nurse, appeared. I told her my latest news. She had already heard it.

"News travels fast around here," I said.

"Like staph infections," she said.

"I feel as though my heart attack is becoming a second banana."

"Oh, no. A heart attack is never a second banana. Heart

disease kills more women than anything else. Did you know that?"

In fact, I did know that. It was a research tidbit gathered for some magazine article I had done years earlier. I could remember neither the magazine nor the article, but I remembered that tidbit. Tons of tidbits, gathered over the years, roll around in my head like unstrung beads. Occupational hazard of the popular-magazine journalist: we become dilettantes on many subjects, masters of none.

(Later I learned another tidbit that temporarily unhinged me: women are more apt than men to have a second heart attack within a year of the first. Learning this, I got a calendar and circled my first-anniversary date, then eleven months down the line, in red highlighter. I began marking off days, laughing at myself even as I did it, which in no way stopped me from doing it. I kept thinking of the old theater joke about the actor who gets a part in a Broadway play. By union rules, the producers have ten days within which to fire him; after that, they can't. He goes home, turns out the lights, lowers the blinds, disconnects the telephone, stuffs rags under the door, and waits. In the final hour of Day Nine, there comes a banging at the door. "Western Union," a voice calls. He sits silent. The voice yells, "I know you're in there. Open up!" More banging. Finally, trembling, he opens the door, rips open the telegram, reads it and gasps. "Thank God!" he cries out. "My mother died!")

And did I know, Carla went on, that, although most women think that breast cancer is their primary killer, heart disease kills more women than all kinds of cancer *combined*?

No, I hadn't known that. That seems remarkable, because as I look up and around in the world familiar to me, it doesn't match what I see. What I see is cancer. My life has been all too full of women friends and relations who have or have had cancer of one sort or another, mainly breast, of course, but I do not happen to know any women, except yours truly, who have had heart attacks. None. It's all men, all men, all men. So that statistic is hard to believe.

Well, it's true. And furthermore, did I know that, although more men have heart attacks, more women die of them?

No. Why should that be?

And that more women than men die before they ever get to the hospital?

Why?

Because they simply don't recognize the symptoms, Carla said. And that is why it's important to know. Because women's heart-attack symptoms can look dramatically different from men's.

For instance, she said, picture this man: He is having a heart attack that is every movie cliché you ever saw. In fact, we call it the Hollywood Heart Attack. His pain is crushing. *Crushing*, just as you always hear it described. He also may have pain or tingling radiating into his arm, probably the left, and maybe into the jaw. He is breathing hard. He is sweating heavily. He feels weak. And he probably has a sense of dread, and astonishment, too, because he just can't believe this is happening to him, nobody ever believes it, but, really, *there can be no doubt.* He calls, or somebody calls, his doctor, or 911, and an ambulance comes *fast*, which is important, because half of all heart-attack victims die within the first half hour if they don't get treated, and he is taken to an emergency room, and he survives.

Now, here is this woman: She may be having (or not) some chest pain, but it is probably not severe, very rarely "crushing," and possibly (or not) she feels nauseated, possibly she is vomiting, possibly she has a sense of heaviness or pressure in her chest, possibly a growing sense of anxiety, even a strange sense of foreboding, and she may also be feeling unfamiliar sensations in other parts of her body—in the arm, or the shoulder, or the back, or some combination—and what does it all add up to? It isn't clear. She doesn't know. And maybe she calls for help, and maybe she does not, and maybe she dies because she didn't know what was happening to her. With women, the symptoms are so . . . *various*, Carla said. And saying this, she struck a pose that is etched permanently in my mind's eye.

She stepped back from the bed in that little room, taking stage center, as it were. A big woman, Carla. Tall, broad, not heavy but ample. She put one hand just below her nose, holding it parallel to the floor, as though in salute, and she put the other hand just below her belly, as though cupping an advanced pregnancy, and she said: "From here to here"—standing, statuelike, with the two hands in position—"*anything* could be a symptom."

Anything. The jaw, the neck, the throat, the mouth, the shoulders, the back, the arms, the chest, the diaphragm, the abdomen.

"That is terrifying," I said.

"It's just information," Carla said. "It's good to be informed, not terrified."

Doubtlessly so. I then asked her the most obvious question: Why should there be these gender differences?

Answer: Nobody really knows.

It's good to be informed, not terrified. It sounded like a proverb to be cross-stitched on a sampler and hung by the bed to give solace through those nights when you feel on information overload.

The chills came back that night. I did not hallucinate again, no more wondering if I was dead, but I did wonder, in a seeming state of calm, as though making dispassionate inquiry into a medically interesting question, if I was dying.

I thought, Since illness is known to lower resistance, and since I have recently had a heart attack, which surely gives a boost to those little buggers within my bloodstream, and since 20 to 40 percent of people with this infection are at risk of dying, even if they do not have lowered resistance, it seems, let us say, not probable but wholly possible, considering the various mortal possibilities, that I may, in this hospital, in this very bed, in the exceedingly near future, kick the bucket.

I thought about medical jargon, how, when a patient suddenly got worse and died, they used to say, "He went bad." Then the jargon had evolved or devolved from bad to sour: "He went sour," which I had always thought was pretty apt. And now the chic term, at least among many of the young residents, seemed to be "He went south," which was even more picturesque. *South.* Would I be going *south*? And, if so, to *which* south? Would it be to Charleston, South Carolina, or to the end of the line?

I contemplated my funeral, on the face of it a ghoulish contemplation, but it actually soothed me, lent me a sense of efficiency.

Who would come to the funeral? Would there be a full house? I must remember to tell Al not to choose too large a venue; it would be so embarrassing to have a scanty house. Not that I would expect SRO, my expectations are not so grand, but I would hope at least for respectable numbers.

Who would deliver the eulogies? My old pal Ann had laid it all out before she died, the program, the music, the order of eulogists, everything. I admired the efficiency of it, but I don't think I would want to do it. Ann knew that she was dying. It was a practical act of anticipation. I do not know that I am dying. I am simply confronting the possibility. For me it would be an unseemly jumping of the gun.

Should I prepare a list of eulogists, or rely on volunteers? A tricky business. I remembered when my old boss Lester Markel, the editor of *The New York Sunday Times*, a legendary ogre who terrified his staff (though I, very young and frivolous, gave him sass, which he liked), died, and they went shopping for eulogists. There were few takers. One was the late, great journalist Tom Wicker, who told me: "I did it because nobody else wanted to. I felt sorry for the old bastard."

These days, a good eulogy seems to require funny anecdotes. I don't know why. I do know that funny anecdotes were not a staple of the funerals of my youth, but that may be because I went, mostly, to Jewish funerals. After the service, you would go to the home of the deceased and, if it was a religiously observant household, the women would be throwing sheets over all the mirrors. The official reason was that in your bereavement you were supposed to withdraw completely from the world, even from your own worldly image, but I have it on good authority that this was just cover for a superstition that persisted from old times in the shtetl, namely, that if you don't drape the mirrors, the ghost of the dead will come out and cause you more grief, of which you've got enough already.

Who would officiate? Hal had not been religious, and no clergyman had officiated at his memorial service. Signs of our secular times: I have heard clergymen officiating at services for people they had never even met and pretending to have known them forever. This can boomerang. When my *Times* colleague Laura died, her family wanted a minister to lead the service, though Laura had never, to my knowledge, entered a house of worship to do any worshipping, and the minister had managed it extremely well, for someone who had never met Laura at all, except that he kept calling her Linda. *And we thank thee, Lord, for the gift of Linda in our lives . . .*

Hal had come from a family in which there were certain cultural inversions. In that clan, the business to be in was show business, and Hal was the black sheep, possibly the only such case in the history of Jewish families, because he was a doctor. At the funeral, his cousin Norman, a pillar of support through the long medical odyssey, had spoken comfortingly of Hal's good and useful life, and his late cousin David, who no one would ever had thought of as having deep feelings of faith, had tearfully recited the Lord's Prayer, and that had been the full extent of religious expression.

I will tell Al: Make it a secular ceremony, please. And should there be a week of secular equivalent to the shiva? Who would come? Would it be a nice party, or an unrelieved downer? My recollection, which is dim, of shiva protocol, is that it's okay to be merry, but not *too* merry. After the service for Hal, the apartment had been mobbed with mourners. People said, "I can't eat" and ate. They said, "Can you believe it? I can't believe it." They said, "What can you do? There is nothing you can do," and shook their heads slowly to convey the depth of their impotence. But they also drank. They also laughed and said, "I will never forget the time that Hal . . ."

Just about everyone said, "At least he wasn't in pain," which is what I've always called the At Least. In mourning we manage always to find either an At Least or an If Only: *At least* he was not in pain; *at least* the doctors did everything possible; *at least* he lived to see his grandchild born. Alternatively: *If only* he had not been in pain; *if only* the doctors had done everything possible; *if only* he had lived to see his grandchild born. And so forth.

The At Least is generally what used to be called WASP territory. I think that we Semites, as a class, tend more toward the If Only. But what I mostly heard them saying about Hal was the At Least, which was nice. If I die, I hope they will say the *At Least* for me. . . .

The chills eased. I felt thirsty and rang for juice. The aide Sam—who morning and evening would fix my bed tenderly, as though the sheets were fragile silks, coaxing out each wrinkle, and then, when the bed was ready, blanket drawn up taut, pillows plumped, would turn, offer a courtly arm to help me out of the turquoise Naugahyde visitors' chair, give me that big sweet smile and say, with unfailing cheer and pride in a job well done, "You're in good hands with Allstate!"—came into the room.

"It was lucky you got that infection while you were here," he said, "so we could take care of you."

And it was, I supposed, very lucky indeed.

But by morning, nobody was talking about lucky.

chapter nine

By morning, I couldn't walk.

My leg. What's the matter with my leg? I can't move my leg.

My arm still throbs, but it is a picnic compared to this leg, what ghastly pain, I have never felt such pain, when I try to lift it, bend it, flex it, simply slide it an inch along the mattress, my God, it is agony, *what's the matter with my leg?*

Nobody knows. If they do, they aren't saying. They shrug. All I know is that just yesterday, a week after a heart attack, I was parading pain-free up and down these corridors, Al and I went walking and my leg was fine—it obeyed orders, it did everything a good leg is supposed to do—and I wake up this morning and suddenly it is a dead thing stretched on the bed. Except that dead things do not cause agony.

Now they've brought me a walker. I remember how I resented the cane. Amended wish list: my kingdom for a cane.

I am a different woman from the woman I was just two days ago. I feel sad and angry, but I don't know whom or what to be angry at. Unfocused anger is not helpful. What helps is to be able to point a finger and say, *The butler did it.* But here, at whom would I point a finger? I don't even know what's wrong.

Of course, this means that I no longer have clear alternatives. The nurse Noreen put it to me cleanly: "If you can't walk, you shouldn't go home."

Stuart came. He sat in the aqua Naugahyde visitors' chair—who chooses aqua Naugahyde? Was there a fire sale? Was there a blind decorator?—sat in that chair and looked glumly at my infected arm, and at the leg that will not move, and shook his head and said, "This is why I wanted you discharged over the weekend. Hospitals are dangerous places."

I have heard that before. Hal used to say it. His colleagues used to say it, in safe surroundings, at dinner tables, never for attribution. To hear it now, as a patient in a hospital room, made a memorable impression.

Stuart said, "Why are you still here?"

"The doctor who covered for you said she couldn't discharge me because something happened."

"What?"

"She said they didn't know. There was a big bump in my EKG and whenever you get a bump like that, it means that something happened."

Stuart shrugged. That is a specialty around here, the shrug.

I said, "She said that she couldn't responsibly discharge me while my signs were so unstable."

Another shrug.

In the next several days, I became a very popular lady. I was no longer a garden-variety cardiac. Now that I had this weird leg, an acute and agonizing condition of unknown etiology with no known solution, I was suddenly an interesting case.

First came Dr. Hearst, the infectious diseases man, for another conference about my bug.

Dr. Hearst does not sit in the aqua Naugahyde chair. He sits on the edge of my bed, as he did before, and this pleases me, as it did before. To me it is not inappropriate. It is avuncular, and avuncular is good. Dr. Hearst knows his customers. Senior citizen that I am, also feminist in good standing, staunch defender of my autonomy, my self-sufficiency, my equality, still: how I do, in some perverse part of myself, still love the old days, with the sweet old melodies, with the sweet old Big Daddy lyrics, "Now, don't you worry your pretty little head, we'll take care of everything . . . "

How soothing. How embarrassing.

But when Dr. Hearst spoke he was no Big Daddy. He was a straight talker, equal to equal, and I liked that part, too.

"Given the condition of your leg, we shouldn't delay treatment," he said. "We should start the antibiotic immediately. The infection may have spread to that leg, possibly into the hip joint. That probably is not the case, but it *could* be, and that would be worrisome. You get a shallow infection, like this," pointing to my arm, "and the antibiotic can reach it easily. But if that infection is deep inside, the antibiotic has a tough time getting to it, getting past bone, and so forth, and it can be very difficult to treat."

"How do we find out if the hip is infected?"

"The only sure test is an MRI (magnetic resonance imaging). But we can't do an MRI on a patient who just had metal installed in her heart."

With this, I entertained an image of magnetic forces sucking the stent out of me as I lay in that tunnel. "So what do we do?"

"There's another test, not as good, but it may yield information. We'll order it."

"And if my leg is not infected, what could be causing the pain?"

"We don't know yet. I understand you have a history of arthritis?"

"Yes."

"It may be you're having a severe arthritic attack. An acute arthritic meltdown."

Oh, come on, Dr. Hearst. Arthritis, sure, a stab here, a spasm there, and after an hour in a car I stand bent as a comma, *Jeez my aching back*, all those standard arthritic complaints, but what does that have to do with this *agony*? "You really think arthritis could explain pain this severe?"

Dr. Hearst regards me with sympathy and impassivity, the prescribed mixed dose. "Let's wait and see," he says, and gives me almost a smile, and is gone.

Next came the consultant I called Liverlips. The man was blameless but also charmless, given to officiousness. As I saw more of him, I understood that it was a cover for insecurity, as officiousness often is, and I liked him better. But in the beginning, I displaced my distaste for him onto his lips—which were, in fact, thick and wet and purple—and called him Liverlips.

"I think you may have a hidden fracture," he said. "I want to schedule an MRI."

"Dr. Hearst was here yesterday. He said I can't have an MRI because of the stent. You can't have an MRI for a year after you get a stent." Contributing my own officiousness.

"Oh, that's an old theory. These days we can do an MRI after . . . How long have you had that stent?"

"Just over a week."

"Oh." He paused. A nurse was in the room. He could not lose ground in front of a nurse. "Well, we'll see. I'll discuss it with the MRI people."

"Please discuss it with Stuart. He's my doctor."

Liverlips's lips tightened, which was, in fact, becoming to him. He nodded curtly to me and left the room.

A hidden fracture? No one else had made such a suggestion. I couldn't understand it. If a fracture was so small, so *mere*, that it could hide from an X-ray, how could it cause so much pain?

Dr. Dalmau, who looked elfin, fragile, was energy efficient and brisk as a cold shower.

"Raise your leg for me," she said.

"I can't."

"Do you mind if I do it?" She raised it slightly—it was the left—and electric shock swept up the length of the leg into the pelvis. I yelped.

She apologized. "Describe the arc of pain," she said.

The Arc of Pain. What a title! Job could have used that title. Plath could have used that title. Also, my late aunt Amelia, an Olympic-scale sufferer, who could go on at remarkable length in this way: "I have two kinds of arthritis and my bones are all gone. My stomach—my worst enemy should not have such a stomach. I am in pain from the minute I wake up until the minute I go to sleep, and I never sleep because of the pain. My doctor says I am a living miracle. It surprises him that I am still alive. Here, have another Danish."

I described the pain as best I could.

The doctor nodded. "Sciatica," she said.

"I've never had sciatica. Why would I suddenly get sciatica?"

"Well, suddenly having a lot of inflammation from your heart attack could have set it off."

"How do you cure it?"

"Rest."

Terrific. As though I have a choice.

She left me with the impression that she was playing a guessing game.

But who wasn't?

The pain got worse. The guessing game went on.

One morning a courtly stranger, wearing a brown suit and an orange tie printed with pink elephants, appeared. He spoke formally, with a faint accent. "How do you do, I am Dr. Glauber, from——." He named an orthopedic group practice where I had been treated for various injuries over the years. "May I see this naughty leg of yours?"

He took hold of my right leg and began swinging it from side to side. "Well, it seems to be moving very nicely," he said.

"It's the other leg."

"Ah. Of course." He swung my left leg. I cried out.

"I am sorry. I will be very careful. If I may . . ." He moved the leg gently. I said, "Please stop. It hurts."

He gave up, sighed, sat down, tented his hands in front of his face. He said, "I think you are suffering from severe muscle spasm. Your arthritis has been aggravated by so much lying in bed, not moving around, not having any exercise. You need to exercise."

"How? I can't walk."

"Ah." We sat in silence, contemplating this dilemma, both of us staring at the floor as though it held answers.

Finally, he said, "Well, I will confer with my colleagues. Good day." He bent slightly from the waist and reached for my hand. For a wild moment, I thought he might kiss it. He shook it and left.

Later that day, Dr. Glauber's colleague appeared. Dr. Clurman, a jolly fellow who, in all the years I had known him, would deliver news, whether good or bad, with a big undifferentiating smile. He smiled now as he said, "We've reviewed all the notes, and the consensus of our group is that your infection has spread to your hip joint."

No, no. Don't tell me that. "But just this morning Dr. Glauber examined me and said it was muscle spasm."

"Hm. Well. Now that we've conferred further, we're pretty sure the hip joint is infected."

"That's not good news."

"No, it's not."

"How do you treat it?"

"Usually, the first step is to wash out the joint before treating it further. With you we can't do that, because washing out a hip joint requires general anesthesia. Given that you just had a heart attack, we'd have to consider"—smiling—"the risk of subjecting you to general anesthesia."

"So?"

"So we wait to see if the antibiotic works. That can take a long time. Best-case scenario, it works. But if it doesn't . . ."

"If it doesn't?" Listen, talk straight. I want to know everything.

And Dr. Clurman says, "If it doesn't, we have a problem." *Houston, we have a problem.* "Then we'd have to sit down with your cardiologist and the surgery guys and figure out what to do. You might need a new hip. And if we can't do that—again, it's the anesthesia problem—do you just live with the pain? It's a tough decision." Big smile. "See you tomorrow." And over and out.

Live with the pain? This, right now, is the first time I have ever thought, *Why me?* Such an absurd question, but now I am asking it. Now I feel panic. *Live with the pain?*

Why the hell did he tell me so much? Truth, yes, but at least pretty it up. Soften the edges. Hal said once, "There are ways and ways to tell the truth. If a patient with a particular type and stage of cancer asks, 'Doc, how long do I have?' you can say, 'Statistically, three to five years.' That's one kind of truth. Or you can say, 'You know, nobody really knows. Statistics really don't mean anything for the individual. Why don't you come back in three years, we'll see how you're doing, and we'll talk about it again.' And that's truth, too."

Once, when I was writing some piece about truth-telling in medicine, about what a conflict-fraught issue it was for doctors and patients alike, Fifi was in the hospital and her husband, Lewis, went to visit her and told me: "There were four beds in the room and in one was this ancient woman who kept crying out all night, and the worst thing was, she was crying for her mother. Can you imagine?"

Oh, yes. I can imagine that woman. I can remember the

old man on the gurney with the Auschwitz face who cried out, just yesterday I think, for his mother.

Live with the pain? *Mama! Mama!*

So here's the deal:

It's an acute arthritic meltdown.

Or it is a hidden fracture.

Or it is severe muscle spasm, caused by exacerbation of arthritis, caused by lack of exercise.

Or it is sciatica, caused by inflammation, caused by a heart attack.

Or it is an infected hip joint. In which case, Houston, we have a problem.

Al loves the muscle-spasm theory. It is logical, reversible, unserious. It's become his mantra: "It's all from lying in one position. If I could just get you home, start you exercising a little . . ."

"Well, I'll be home for Christmas, anyway."

"That's six weeks from now." He looked unrelievedly sad.

"And maybe they'll spring me for Thanksgiving dinner."

"That would be nice."

"But you'd have to promise to sign me back in by curfew."

"What happens if I don't? They arrest me?"

"I turn into a pumpkin."

He refused to be humored. I said, "At least I showed good timing."

"What do you mean?"

"Getting sick now. So now you won't have to go to any of those big holiday parties."

Now he did smile wanly. He hates big parties. He is so like Hal in this way. Quiet men, composed, centered. Not small-talkers. Not glad-handers. Both, so unlike me, efficient and resolute. Both with that rocklike solidity, what the Brits call "bottom." You're in Good Hands with Allstate.

Well, how could it be otherwise? They would of course be alike. They would of course both be efficient and resolute. They would of course both have *bottom*, bottom being what I lacked, and needed, and always would manage to find.

We repeat ourselves instinctively, those of us who couple more than once. We move like bird dogs toward the same visceral types. They may look different on the outside, but there is some essential sameness within. Almost always.

Among the doers and the talkers, I have always been

more of a talker. And twice fell in love, no accident, with major doers. A perfect compensatory arrangement: I could do the chatting for them and they could do the heavy lifting for me. This is how love happens. This is my Law of Compensatory Mechanisms.

Whatever else it may be, love is also a compensatory mechanism. This is a theory based on a broad foundation of no scientific evidence whatever, but just look around. See what people do. The burgher falls for the dreamer, the loner marries the mixer; we all, knowingly or not, seek someone who can do for us what we cannot do for ourselves.

These two dear men of mine, if we were beds, they would be beds made with hospital corners and I would be an unmade bed. I loosened them up a little, they tidied me up a little—it *worked*.

Take almost any couple. Take one of the partners into a room, go slow, go easy, ask about their habits of work and leisure, their hobbies, their friends, their kids, and if you've asked the right questions, you'll find the answer: how the Law works for that couple.

Of course, a compensatory mechanism is not *necessarily* a healthy mechanism, which is why the prude falls for the philanderer and the masochist falls for the sadist, and so forth, and if the sadist exits the picture, either on foot or in a box, the masochist will very likely find another sadist. We need what we need.

I understand that. What I do not understand is the perversity of my own needs. Why should I, a woman who has always been independent in most of the practical ways of life, able and eager to make her own way, earn her own way, live her own way, unshy with men in business and in bed—why should I still feel, lurking deep within me, such perverse dependencies and take such perverse pleasure from the thought of being protected by men, cosseted by men, sustained and safeguarded by men?

Not an uncommon perversity. We used to talk about it a lot in my old consciousness-raising group, back in the '70s and '80s. We would organize and we would march and we would demonstrate and then we would sit in our CR sessions and parse our own inconsistencies. Lessons learned at Mother's knee.

One of the group, a woman who had finally walked out of a long, miserable marriage, once said, "I would never admit it outside of this room, but sometimes I get *so sick* of taking care of myself."

We all laughed in horror, covering our mouths like geishas, and someone else said, "You can't *mean* that." But I thought she did, sort of. I had been widowed not long before, and I understood it. In times of fear or foreboding, such as then, such as now, there is a fallback position, and the fallback position is men.

You're in Good Hands with Allstate.

I wonder if maybe some of the younger ones feel it too, and just don't talk about it.

I was jolted out of these thoughts by a visit from Stuart.

Stuart said that he has a theory.

His theory was that I did not have a heart attack.

chapter ten

Takotsubo.

That was Stuart's theory: that was what had happened to me. A strange, rare, esoteric condition nobody had ever heard of, including people in the medical community, until 1990, when it had first been isolated, in Japan, and named for the octopus pot, the pot Japanese fishermen use to trap octopuses, which has a narrow neck and a bulbous body, rather like the old standard lightbulb, and which is what the human heart resembles when it is beset by this strange, rare, esoteric condition that nobody had ever heard of, including people in the medical community, and most assuredly including me.

Stuart was elated. How could it have been a heart attack? The most recent pictures of my heart, taken just yesterday, just a week after the event, looked almost normal. "Like the heart of a kid! Pumping like crazy!"

Hearts, if they recover from heart attacks, are not supposed to recover this quickly. But from takotsubo, yes! In weeks, in days from the onset of the attack—total recovery!

"It's fascinating," he said. "They first found it in these high-powered Japanese businessmen who work under tremendous stress. What happens is, in reaction to the stress, the heart virtually strangles itself, and it looks just like a heart attack, but then it reverts to a perfectly normal state. I think that's what happened to you. You should look it up. It's amazing. It's the most dramatic example you can imagine of the mind-body connection."

Takotsubo cardiomyopathy . . . is a type of non-ischaemic cardiomyopathy in which there is a sudden temporary weakening of the myocardium (the muscle of the heart). Because this weakening can be triggered by emotional stress, such as the death of a loved one, a break-up, or constant anxiety, the condition is also known as Broken Heart Syndrome . . .

—*Wikipedia*

Broken heart syndrome is a temporary heart condition brought on by stressful situations, such as the death of a loved one. People with broken heart syndrome may have sudden chest pain or think they're having a heart attack.

These broken heart syndrome symptoms may be brought on by the heart's reaction to a surge of stress hormones. In broken heart syndrome, a part of your heart temporarily enlarges and doesn't pump well. . . . The symptoms of broken heart syndrome are treatable, and the condition usually reverses itself in about a week.

—*The Mayo Clinic*

"But what about the stress, Stuart?" Looking back, seeing myself sitting in the kitchen, eating the soup, making the list of clothes to pack for the birthday trip to Charleston. "I wasn't under any stress."

"Oh, you probably were. Everyone has stress. Maybe it was just the stress of your gastric upset."

He was excited, revved up. I sensed something of a Sherlock Holmesian high here, but something else, too. Stuart, dear Stuart, are you just possibly, and most surely out of consciousness, feeling a little bit guarded, a little bit wary, a little bit in need of self-justification, in the wake of having missed the call on your patient's heart attack? (If the attack didn't happen, the call wasn't missed. Q.E.D.)

I half-wanted to say: Listen, if you're feeling any of the above, please don't. I do not remotely blame you, I had atypical symptoms, it was an easy call to miss, and all's well that ends well.

The other half told me to keep my mouth shut, which, whenever in doubt, is a good idea.

I tried the takotsubo theory out on several of the consultants on my case.

One said, "Tako what? Never heard of it."

Another said, with a *tch* of reproach, as though I was presenting the theory on my own, "But you had an *occluded artery*. You have a *stent* in you. Do you think we put those in for the *fun* of it?"

Takotsubo had no takers.

Stuart brought up the subject once or twice more ("I know you don't believe me," he said), and then he let it go. Or, at least, seemed to let it go.

What was in his own heart I couldn't know.

"Hi! How's everything going?"

It was the nurse practitioner Carla, looking and sounding perky.

"I don't know," I said.

"What do you mean?"

"I'm confused. And kind of—"

"Depressed? Feeling a little depressed, Martha?

"No, I don't think so. Not depressed."

Not that I will say this to you, Carla, but I damn well know I'm not depressed. Depression is not my style. In the last year of Hal's life, as he kept sliding inevitably downward, I thought sometimes, and found great comfort in the thought, Well, now, maybe I'll just lie down beside him and we can bow out together. I know which pills would do the job.

But I knew that I would never do it. I would never do it because I am not basically a depressive type, I tend more toward the hysteric. And for hysterics tomorrow is precious, because there is always something else to get hysterical about.

"Not depressed. I think I'm kind of . . . angry."

"Angry? Can you tell me why, Martha?" Tiptoeing around it, knowing the answer full well.

"Well, it's just so . . . so *frustrating*. I have this heart attack and I'm told that it's not mild, it's worse than a mild attack, *not massive but not mild*, that's exactly what he said, but then I make this terrific recovery, that's what I'm told, and I'm supposed to be going home in three days and everyone keeps congratulating me for making such a terrific recovery, because a heart attack that's worse than a mild attack, or maybe even any kind of heart attack, is a really big deal, right?"

Right. Carla nods emphatically.

"Then I get this big-deal infection . . . that's what they always say, that I *got* this infection, like it's *my fault* . . ."

And now I'm skidding down Memory Lane again, remembering the unfrivolous game that Hal called "It's Your Fault," as in:

Patient: Why did the surgery take so long?
Doctor: Because you lost a lot of blood. *Not: Because I botched the surgery.*

Echoes of Heartsounds

Patient: Why did this break mend so badly?

Doctor: Because you got too active. *Not: Because the cast was applied incorrectly.*

Patient: Why was I infected?

Doctor: Because your resistance was low. *Not: Because our sanitation protocols are not good enough.*

". . . and now my heart seems to be fine, *almost normal,* they tell me, but now I can't walk and I have the worst pain I've ever had in my life and nobody can say why and the ortho-pedist says I may have to live with it and I've got to stay in this bed for four more weeks because of an infection that is a *hospital-acquired infection,* it is *not my fault*"—sniffling now—"and suddenly the heart attack is the supporting act in the show, it's the warm-up, it's a kind of nonevent, it's the only damn heart attack I ever heard of that. . ."

"No, no. Listen to me. I've told you, a heart attack is *never* a nonevent. . . ."

". . . and now my doctor is telling me that I didn't even *have* a heart attack. It was something called tako . . . tako . . ."

This stops her cold. She doesn't know what to do with this. Inside her head she is fumbling, I can feel her fum-bling. Finally, she chooses what is really her only possible choice, which is to duck it.

"Listen, I understand your anger and I don't blame you," she says.

I understand your anger and I don't blame you: that is really all that is required, in the way that a child requires *"You did a naughty thing, but I still love you."* But then she says, "You know what I do when I feel blue? I go to this little place in my neighborhood, and I get my hair done and I get a manicure, the whole thing costs me just $35, and then I feel so much better. We can bring someone in. Would you like to have a manicure?"

A manicure. I am tempted to be churlish, but in fact I should be glad. These are the so-called soft issues in medicine, as opposed to the hard, or clinical, issues.

Hard issues: the medical names of the eleven little bones of the wrist. "It's a terrible education," I can remember Hal saying. "It's all about body parts. They teach you nothing about *people.*"

Soft issues: the communication issues; the bedside-manner issues; the "How are your spirits?" issues that they never used to pay any attention to at all. In the five years of his own many hospitalizations, no doctor ever asked Hal, "How are your spirits?"

So this is progress. Be thankful.

No manicure, I say, but thanks for asking.

Carla says, "Sometimes it helps to talk to someone. Would you like to see a chaplain?"

No, thanks.

"Do you feel better now?"

"Yes."

"Still angry?"

"No."

But that is a lie.

I am still angry. Tell me what has or has not happened to my heart and what has or has not happened to my leg and tell me why, out of the whole vast armamentarium of this place, there is nothing better to offer than a shave and a haircut, two bits.

Or at least tell me the word I would be grateful to hear: *Sorry.*

"That staph that hit you is a *very nasty customer,*" Dr. Hearst said. Agreed. But did it hit me? How did it hit me? Did it fly in through a window and hit me? Everyone has *tch-tch*ed over this *very nasty customer* of mine, everyone has offered commiseration, everyone has offered reassurance, but what no one has offered is an apology. Nothing elaborate. Just a few spirit-soothing words on the order of: we're sorry that it happened in our institution, or that it happened in our care, or even that it might be called, in some communal, non-finger-pointing way, *our fault* . . .

But no, none of the above. I think it is a professional tic, a lesson learned not formally but absorbed through the pores: Never Admit Fault. Which is understandable enough when there has been some colossal baroque mistake, the kind that makes lawyers' mouths water, such as removing the wrong organ, or delivering a fatal dose of medication. But in this case, why all the tiptoeing around? Hospital-acquired infection, garden-variety problem, doubtless happens in every hospital in the country; it's not malpractice—somebody simply neglected to wash hands, or didn't adequately disinfect some injection site, or didn't something-or-other. You'll never know what. You'll never know who.

And to be totally fair, if I must be totally fair, which I am in no mood to be, but let me force myself, they probably don't know themselves.

I think of the clumsy show-offy kid who said, "That left anterior artery of yours, the one that occluded . . . You know what we call that one? We call it the Widow Maker." That was far too much information. But what is worse, too much or not enough? Not enough, not enough, not enough! That is what is terrifying. What is terrifying is ignorance.

Am I sure of that? If I had Alzheimer's disease, would I want to be told? If I had incontestably terminal cancer, would I want to be told? It is not an easy thing to know. Not easy for the patient and, let us not forget, not easy for the doctor, who understands full well the patient's rich ambivalences.

On the one hand: Don't play God with me. Treat me like a responsible adult. Tell me everything. I want the truth.

On the other: Be God. I don't ask to know, I don't need to know, I don't want to know *nothin'*. Just make me well.

And both, with absolute simultaneity.

I feel that everything keeps getting more complicated, layers of uncertainty piling up and up, like a wave building ever higher before crashing on the shore. What I can't figure out is, am I the wave, or am I the shore?

Al came then, as I lay in bed gazing with an angry eye at the wheelchair that sat in the corner. He said, "Let's go for a ride," and helped me into the chair, which was in itself a laborious undertaking, and steered me out of the room, and suddenly there we were; my husband Al was wheeling me through these very same corridors where I had so often, over several years, wheeled my husband Hal, and I began to cry.

I understood that I was in fact crying not simply for the loss of Hal, as though that had been just yesterday, but also in a sense for the loss of me, my soundness of body, and for Al's loss of a sound-bodied wife, and crying too for loss itself, for anyone's loss, the very idea of loss, all the irretrievabilities that face us.

I thought, The past is too much here, it is all too entangled, I can't spend another month amid these memories. Can I talk to Al about this? Will it upset him? Would I care if his thoughts were as much with Judy as mine are with Hal? I hope not, but I don't know. I don't have the courage to bring it up to him.

He stopped the chair and said, "Why are you crying?"

"Hal. When I used to take him out like this in the wheelchair. I keep thinking about Hal."

"I know," he said.

"You do?"

"Of course."

"Does it bother you?"

"Of course not."

Whereupon I cried harder and felt better.

chapter eleven

The bug is in retreat!

All the theories, the sciatica and the acute arthritic meltdown and the hidden fracture and all the others, they are still on the table, and the Mystery of the Naughty Leg remains (and would remain) unsolved. But it does seem self-evident: if antibiotics are curing me, the infection was what crippled me. And I am extraordinarily lucky that the IV treatment worked.

After two weeks of treatment the leg is beginning to behave like a proper limb again. When I am in no motion, I am in no pain. You might say that horizontally, I've made great progress. Vertically, not so great—when I move, the pain is still awful. But I *can* move. I take baby steps, like an old-time geisha with bound ankles. I remember all too vividly when I couldn't get from my bed to the portable commode, which is a couple of yards away, never mind to the bathroom, and had to ask for the bedpan, which distressed me unreasonably. A fine device, the homely bedpan, but as metaphor, it's a killer.

Each day, I push laboriously ahead with the walker, with the zippy young physiotherapist urging me on like a sideliner at the Marathon, *Come on, Martha, keep going, just a little farther, a little bit farther* . . . and then I collapse with gratitude and exhaustion into the wheelchair. The previously loathsome wheelchair is now my new best friend.

The longer I lie in this bed, the younger the doctors get. This morning one of them came in, with his blond baby curls and his smooth baby face, and it was as though he were playing Doctor. A venerable game. I wonder if kids still play Doctor. I remember when I used to play Doctor.

I was five. I played the game with my best friend, Barbara, who lived next door. We alternated roles, one of us the doctor, one the patient. We would go into her bedroom, which had twin beds with bunnies carved into the maple headboards, and the patient would lie down on a bed and shed her panties and spread her legs, and the doctor would take her temperature by inserting a toothpick into her vagina. Luckily, we never caused damage.

Sometimes, another five-year-old, Sharon, would play the game with us. Then the cast was doctor, patient, and nurse. We always stuck Sharon with the patient's role, and on those occasions Barbara and I would fight, quite bitterly, over who would be the doctor. We understood, even at that age, where the power lay.

"Getting a little stir-crazy?" the social worker Phoebe said.

And then some. I hadn't smelled fresh air in a month.

"Okay. It's a beautiful day. Let's go for a stroll."

The three of us, she and the wheelchair and I, took an elevator down, rolled through a lobby and emerged onto the street.

Brilliant sky, cloudless. Light luminous. Trees bare, limbs etched black against pure cobalt. Air to pull in deep and get drunk on. Everything, everyone, in sharpest silhouette.

It stunned me. The strangeness of these familiar sights,

the larger-than-life gorgeousness of it all. I remembered Hal describing the ecstasy of a patient who had been to the very brink and come back. "Doc," he had cried, "I never realized the sky was so blue!"

The rapture of redemption, Hal had called it. As in a psalm, as in a psychoanalytic case history: the Rapture of Redemption.

You cannot describe rapture. How would you describe an orgasm? Pain is very easy to describe. Like a knife thrust into the groin (hip issue). Like an electrical current running down the leg (scoliosis issue). Like a thumb on fire (arthritis issue). But pleasure is hard.

Of course, the rapture never lasted, Hal had said. Give it a few weeks, a few months at most, they would all come down to earth. I was certain that was true. I was also certain, as the wonder of the world hit me on a frenetic street corner on the Upper East Side of Manhattan, with the horns honking and the ambulance sirens shrieking and the street vendors flacking their fajitas and the dog walkers waiting with their plastic baggies while their dogs squatted in the gutter, that the rapture would last for me forever. Anyone who has ever felt the Rapture of Redemption has been certain that it would last forever.

We rolled along the avenue for several blocks and then

rolled back into the hospital through a different entrance, and up a different elevator, and along different corridors, and we were rolling along and I was feeling just fine, still high off that sun, that air, that world seen anew, and suddenly, there it was, staring me in the face: the waiting room. The room where we, his children and his cousins and I, had waited, through the interminable hours of Hal's last night, for him to die.

The Waiting Room, the place to wait for death and hope for redemption. Outfitted to essential specifications: the soothing colors, the hanging landscape, the television set, the Kleenex boxes, the works. Does any room hold more forlorn hope than a hospital waiting room? The walls are damp with it, the air reeks of it, and now it sweeps me backward into the most unwelcome of the memories.

I am back in this room on that night. We sit by that south wall, right there, his daughter, Judith, slumped against me like a boneless creature. His cousins Norman and David are sitting across the room. Norman's wife, Frances, is on the other side of me. Opposite her are two strangers who look like sisters, possibly twins, sharing a Kleenex box. Their eyes are swollen, their nostrils are red, crumpled tissues fill their laps.

Somewhere else, down some hall, behind some swinging doors, he lies through that wretched night, comatose, with doctors saying "Dr. Lear, can you hear me?" which he cannot, and "Dr. Lear, squeeze my hand," which he does not, and sticking pins into him to test for some motor reaction, which at first they think there may be and then they think not.

Norman watches for a time through the glass-paneled swinging doors. Norman sees them do these things. Norman tells us afterward, and repeats it two days later in his eulogy, that at one point he was certain he saw Hal raise an arm and he thought, Norman says, that that was Hal the doctor—to his very end, the doctor—trying to tell them what to do.

It goes on like that through the night and then, soon after dawn, they say to us, "If you want to see him, you must come right now."

I ask, "Would he know me?" and they say, "No, he would not," so I do not go in, but the others go in, and when Judith comes out, she is weeping very bitterly and she says, "That wasn't Daddy," so I am glad I didn't go in.

(It haunted me for years: Had he had any shred of consciousness left? Might he have heard me say good-bye? They had assured me not, but they didn't know for certain, they can never know for certain, not until the heart stops beating, whether anything at all is getting through.)

And minutes later, one of them, a young resident with a perennially sad face, his head shaking with helplessness and regret, appears in the doorway of the waiting room and says nothing but makes the most poignant gesture, simply makes that sweeping *X* gesture with his arms that they do when the boxer has been down for the full count and the referee is declaring the fight over.

And that was it. Hal's fight was over.

And just like that, with that single sweeping *X* gesture, these were his fatherless children and I was his widow. And we all went back to the apartment and sat for a while, staring into our cups of cold coffee, and then Norman and I went into a corner to compose an obit for *The New York Times*.

I recall doing that in a state of utter calm, which was possible, of course, for the same reason that such states of utter calm are always possible: because of the accompanying state of advanced disbelief. Because the reality of being the widow Lear seemed as preposterous to me then as it seemed to me now, as I sat in a wheelchair in that damned waiting room, to be the cardiac Lear.

When we got back to my own room, Stuart was waiting.

I said, "It's so hard to be a patient in this place. The ghosts are in every corner."

He said, "Still ghosts? Even after all this time, Martha?"

Oh, Stuart dear, yes. Even after all this time. Like yesterday.

chapter twelve

Yesterday. Light-years ago, ten minutes ago, as these things always are.

Some specimen he was. Splendidly built ("Amazing," a cardiologist said to me once, very late in the game, "to find an end-stage heart in the body of an Adonis!"), exudations of health, no sign of the nicotine-soaked sludge coating his arteries, no sign of the bloodlines that had made him a genetic patsy in any case, nicotine or no; his father, grandfathers, uncles all done in by their hearts in their sixties, several in their fifties, falling down left and right, off the limbs of a family tree that was eerily like my own. (Our pooled genes might have made a disaster area; just as well, perhaps, that we never had children.)

His face. It has always mattered greatly to me how a man looks, which has never stopped me from resenting that it matters so greatly to men how a woman looks. But there it is: it mattered.

From the first time I met him, before I knew a thing about the man, I was besotted with the face. A craggy sort of face, cleft chin, nobly hooked slender nose, high jutting brow, a profile that might have come off an old Roman coin. Intensely blue eyes narrowed, as though listening hard, or forever figuring the odds. But the craggy face turned shy, with a great sweetness of expression about the eyes and the mouth when he came closer and said, "Martha?" It seemed to me simply the best sort of face a man could have.

This was at my desk, in the old New York Times building on West Forty-Third Street. It was a meeting that had been arranged by mutual friends who had insisted, despite our mutual disinterest, that we would have so much in common.

In fact, we wouldn't have seemed to have much of anything in common. We were living ninety miles and worlds apart.

He was a doctor with a busy practice in Hartford, Connecticut, a midsized (population, back then, 162,000) city ringed by bedroom suburbs, financially dominated by the insurance industry, and frisky as might be expected of a city popularly known as the "Insurance Capital of the World."

He had finished his medical training in New York, at the great institution where I was now a patient. He had loved this place. For him, it had been not simply a hospital but the brick manifestation of all that he held holy, being still an undiluted idealist (which wouldn't last; it doesn't last for any of them): the concept of service, the alleviation of suffering, the stately cadences of the Hippocratic Oath, with its grand "Do No Harm"—a lot of freight for a building to bear.

His boss, the renowned chief of the urology department, was taken with this earnest young man who had gone through Yale under the Jewish quota (such quotas were common in Ivy League schools through the '50s), paying his way by tutoring other students, and had similarly paid his way through medical school, and who now was showing impressive surgical skills. When the three-year residency was finished, he offered Hal a job in the department: Someday, he said, I'll be gone and maybe *you'll* be the next chief of urology.

It was the kind of offer that a newly minted doctor might be expected to kill for.

Hal turned it down. By that time he was married, with a small child, and another on the way, and said that he didn't want his children growing up in these concrete canyons. He wanted them to grow where the green grass grew.

It was a sentiment he shared with millions of young American parents. It was built into the bones of that postwar era. In the 1950s, when families that prayed together were believed to stay together, and the products being endlessly flacked on television were not pain pills and penile aids but floor waxes and baby shampoos, in those '50s, if you weren't raising your kids in the suburbs, where the green grass grew, you weren't raising them right.

There was plenty of grass in Connecticut. There was also the offer of a partnership in a private urology practice, which he accepted.

The young family moved to the pretty suburb of West Hartford, to a street filled with children playing street games and lined with split-level houses in which mothers kept house. It was, like such places all across America, what the writer Robert Paul Smith had once called "the suburban dream incarnate": upscale, white, clean, safe. Nobody thought to tell a child never to talk to strangers.

The dream was interrupted briefly by the Korean War (as a naval officer, his noblest war contribution, Hal said, was dispensing condoms to the crew whenever they left the ship for shore leave). Then he came home to his family and his medical practice.

The practice flourished. The marriage did not. Late in the '50s, the couple was divorced and he took a bachelor apartment nearby. Their children, a nine-year-old girl and an eleven-year-old boy, lived with their mother (it was not an era when courts looked kindly on paternal custody) and were with him for vacations and weekends, squabbling, as children of divorce do, to have sleepovers alone with Daddy.

It was on the cusp of the cataclysmic transformations that would come with the civil rights movement, with the resurgent women's movement, with the anti–Vietnam War movement, with the availability of The Pill—all these streams of social protest and self-assertion converging in a raging river of antiauthoritarianism—and then the divorce rate began to soar, and that was the beginning of the end of the suburban dream incarnate.

Hal began trying to reshape his personal life. He was forty, which meant middle-aged back then, and he later recalled wondering, *A forty-year-old guy, divorced, with children, who the hell would want me?* "And you know what?" he said in true amazement, for he had always been on the shy side, never a ladies' man, "You know what? They all did!"

Including me.

I was in my late twenties—an extremely, possibly irredeemably, advanced age for a nice Jewish girl from Boston to be unmarried. My mother fretted.

I had fled from a pleasant but banal suburban girlhood to this city that I loved, and had a job that I loved, and a life that I loved, moving freely about town and dating various young men, all of us fueled by hormones and ambition, and marriage was nowhere on my agenda. It has become rooted deep in the national myth that a true sexual revolution happened when the decade exploded, just a few years later, but I don't think that our behavior changed all that dramatically. Attitudes changed, not behavior. We simply went public with it.

It was an exciting time for a young woman who was ignorant of gender liabilities, totally ignorant of what would come to be called "women's issues," to be working at a great newspaper. I had never heard of "women's issues." In 1960, who had? If someone had mentioned the phrase to me, I probably would have assumed they were talking about menstruation.

Simone de Beauvoir's pioneering book *The Second Sex* had appeared a decade earlier in France, but was known on this side of the Atlantic only to academics and intellectuals, and I was neither. Betty Friedan's great world changer, *The Feminine Mystique*, would not be published for another several years. I was sailing joyously, mindlessly along at *The Times*, oblivious to the paucity of women editors and writers, except in those ghettos that were designated "women's pages"—Fashion, Food, Home, and Parent & Child.

I worked for *The Sunday Magazine* (now called *The New York Times Magazine*). In newspaper offices today, those that still exist, reporters and editors sit in little carrels staring at computer screens and mumbling to themselves, and it is generally as exciting as a dentist's waiting room. But back then, we all worked in huge open spaces called bullpens, dense with cigarette smoke and the clatter of typewriters and the unrestrained expression of strong feelings. (I remember especially the strong feelings of a great staff writer, Gilbert Millstein. Millstein made paper airplanes. Each winter, at the very moment when the boss, the incomparable ogre Lester Markel, was scheduled to depart on a flight to the Caribbean, Millstein would take an airplane out of his desk drawer, set it afire and send it soaring, briefly and gloriously, to its demise, to the accompaniment of thunderous applause.)

On the entire editorial staff, there were just four women: a staff writer—older (*ancient*, she seemed to me, perhaps in her fifties), scornful of other women, of the type we would later come to call an "Aunt Tom"—a researcher, an assistant picture editor, and me. I was a copy editor, tasked with taking raw manuscripts and doing whatever had to be done to make them fit for publication.

At some point, I discovered that the three other copy editors, who were doing precisely the same job as I, and doing it no better, were earning twice as much. Indignant, I went to the boss, Markel. The men all feared and loathed him. I liked him because he liked me—in part, I think, because I was cheeky with him—and he liked my work. So I made my case with what I look back on now as the self-assurance of an idiot.

Markel stared at me in genuine bewilderment. Why would I be so upset? How could I not understand?

"But they are *men*," he said. "They are *married*. They have *families* to support."

To this day it shames me to recall what I said. I said: "Oh."

As in *Oh, yeah. Of course.* And saw nothing illogical in his reasoning or in my own until a decade later, when I joined a women's consciousness-raising group and found that almost everyone had a similar story to tell.

Instead of a raise, they began giving me small writing assignments, for which I had nagged. I did these on my own time, was paid for them on a freelance basis, and actually considered myself to have come out ahead.

At one point, I believed that nothing on earth could persuade me to give up that job, for it was not just a job. It was a way of being in the world, a reconceiving of possibilities for a daughter of that pleasant but uneventful suburban life; a re-creating of me.

Then I met the man who lived a light-year away, in the Insurance Capital of the World.

He was less than eager for this meeting because he was seeing a woman in Hartford. (Years later, when he died, she sent me an exquisite letter of condolence that broke both our hearts, hers in the writing, mine in the reading. It began: "Dear Ms. Lear, I was the woman in Hal's life when he met you . . .")

I was less than eager because what would one want, after

all, with a man from out of town? But the mutual friends kept at it, as dedicated matchmakers will, and we agreed to meet for a drink.

So there he was, approaching my desk at *The Times*. I remember looking up, seeing the stranger coming slowly toward me, seeing the face, and thinking, *I hope that's him*.

We went to a bar on Eighth Avenue called Downey's, an actors' hangout. We sat in a corner booth. I felt nervous, though I usually didn't with men. I wanted terribly for him to like me, and was prepared to ask the questions that men generally liked to be asked, and then to listen. That was how it was supposed to go: the women would invite the men to talk about themselves, and the men would do so, and the women would listen. That was the protocol.

But not with this man. He asked and he listened. I would learn soon that he had a gift for listening. It was like an ear for music, or an eye for design. (At his memorial service, one of the eulogists would say, "I've known men who loved all mankind but they weren't too good with individuals. Hal didn't spend much time loving all mankind, but oh, how he could connect with individuals! He *listened* like nobody else I've ever known.")

He said, "Tell me about your work."

I babbled on, about how much I loved my job, and how shocked I had been to learn of the gender/wage gap, but when you thought about it, those married men with wives and children to support, it seemed only fair, didn't he agree?

And he, with those cobalt-blue eyes fixed on me, said, "No. I don't agree. Equal work, equal pay."

We sat in that booth until closing time. I remember little else of what we said. It didn't matter. What mattered, of course, was what we didn't say. Nobody past adolescence falls in love at first sight, not really. But that other thing, that electrical current that starts zapping along the neural pathways, making the throat dry, making the heartbeat quicken and the adrenaline flow—that is always immediate.

He had thick dark hair, almost black, not a gray strand in it, set over pure white sideburns. I had wondered momentarily, *Could it be a hairpiece?*—but no, at one point he raked a hand through that hair and pulled up on it, hard, as though to pull an idea out of his skull, and I saw that it was unmistakably his own. (In fact, it was a genetic tic.)

Later, he reached that hand across the table and laid it flat, palm down, fingers spread wide, tip of the middle finger barely touching my own. We stared at our two hands. His was large and well formed, prominently knuckled, with fingertips slightly splayed, a detail I recalled years later when I learned that splayed fingertips were considered a possible marker for heart disease.

I lived on the East Side in the Murray Hill district, a half mile from *The Times*. He walked me home. There was no suggestion of a *nightcap*, a word that, in those days, was a kind of code for sex. There was a tacit understanding that whatever was brewing here, it was too important to be rushed.

He said, "What are you doing next Saturday?"

I said, "Having dinner with you."

He laughed. He put his hand with its splayed fingertips lightly to my cheek. We said good night, and then I went up to my apartment, the skin of my cheek tingling all the way, and called my best friend and told her that I was in love.

She said, "I've never heard you say that before."

I said, "Neither have I."

Three months later he pinned me against a wall in his apartment, a place piled high with the disorder of his bachelor enthusiasms—his sculpting supplies, his ski gear, his travel books—and said, "Enough of this crapping around. When are we going to get married?"

I panicked. Were it playing out today, it would be easy: he would live in his town and I would live in mine, and we would live a weekend life together, a common enough arrangement now. But back then, no. I never considered it. He would never have settled for it. We were both so much of our time.

But to sacrifice my job? For anyone who wanted to work in journalism, there could not have been any place more desirable than *The New York Times*. My women friends, all of whom had careers and high ambition, said, "You're going to quit that job? How terrible!" By which they did not mean that I shouldn't quit the job. They meant, *What bad luck that you must. But, of course, you must.*

And it made my heart ache, but there was no choice, really. I loved him too much.

I said to my mother, "I have news for you."

She wept with joy. Then: "Is he Jewish?"

When I took him to Boston to meet the family, from her cedar hope chest, she withdrew an envelope wrapped in white tissue and presented it, shyly and with great dignity, to the husband-to-be. Inside was a sheet of prescription paper from the man who had been our family doctor for thirty years. It read:

To Whom It May Concern:

This is to certify that I have examined Martha Lucille Weinman, age six, and found her to have a ruptured hymen, probably caused by a fall from a chair as an infant.

Louis Silver, M.D.

It had lain chastely in her hope chest, this small white hope, for twenty-two years, awaiting the moment.

At *The Times*, they gave me a farewell party. They gave me four sets of silver salt-and-pepper shakers. I still have them, stowed in a closet with the silver chafing dishes and the silver pickle forks and the silver sugar tongs. Best of all, they gave me a contract to write for *The Sunday Magazine* as a regular contributor.

We were married in the spring and I moved up to the Insurance Capital of the World.

Echoes of Heartsounds

*   *   *

By those old Freudian yardsticks, work and love, my life could not have been better.

I was finishing a book that would be published months later. It was based on an article I had done for *The Times*, about parents who compete for status through their children (a theme that is resurrected in every generation, always as though brand-new). It wasn't a good book, really—a glib critique of overinvolved parents, written by a woman who never herself had paid the dues of parenthood—but it seemed to hit a nerve, and got a lot of media coverage, and became a bestseller. So there was all that ego-feeding flurry.

And I was now doing several articles a year for *The Sunday Magazine*. Often they were profiles that involved travel, which I loved—having claim to the big *Of* (". . . Martha Lear *of The New York Times*"), and the expense accounts, being courted by publicists, flying to Los Angeles first-class—luxuries that are gone, all gone, in this era of a struggling print-magazine industry—and interviewing movie stars in the Polo Lounge.

So my professional life was marvelous.

And my personal life was almost marvelous.

We bought an old house in a picture-book town, countrified and sunny, with land plentiful enough to be called grounds. There were low stone walls, and birch-thick woods sloping gently downward toward a lake where neighbors swam in summer and skated in winter. Midway down to the lake, nestled beneath the birches, was a tiny log cabin. I had thought to use it as a studio, but one day, I saw a snake there, harmless but a snake nonetheless, and that was the end of that.

We put in a pool. Poolside was where we were lazing one Sunday afternoon, the Sunday *Times* spread between us, when a stranger rapped at the gate. A woman, in her forties, palpably nervous.

"I used to own this house," she said, looking at her feet.

We invited her in and she told us her story, sitting straight as an angle iron, looking only downward, with her hands kneading each other in her lap. She and her husband had gone to high school together, had never dated anyone but each other, had moved as newlyweds into this house, had raised their two children in this house, had lived a joyous life in this house, and he had planted those pink dogwoods, and he had built those stone walls, and he had built that log cabin down there as a playhouse for the kids, and then he had gone off to the Korean War and been killed.

We sat stunned. She was crying silently. Hal's eyes were brimming. Finally, he saved the moment. "Tell us about the children," he said, and listened in that way of his, and when she had regained her composure we took her through the house, and then, because she asked to go there, down to the little cabin in the woods.

She knew precisely what she wanted to see. Immediately upon entering the cabin, she swung the door wide open and stood peering at the wood-paneled wall behind it. There, in faint pencil markings, were the growth charts of children. I had to look away from what was in her face.

Come back any time, bring the children, we told her.

We never saw her again.

Fifteen years later, a year widowed, I would be visiting friends in West Hartford, and would find myself driving out to the house and, with my heart pounding but following some impulse that would not be denied, I became that nervous stranger, inching down that long driveway and backing into a spot by the tree that bisected the macadam, which I could have done with my eyes closed, and rapped at the door and said to the man who opened it, "I used to own this house."

The owners took me through it, as Hal and I had taken our guest. They had it changed it substantially, for which I was both glad and saddened, but they had not changed the pool area, where I found what we had scratched like a pair of besotted adolescents into the wet cement of the brand-new poolside, a lifetime ago: two hearts, "H. L. loves M. L." and "M. L. loves H. L.", with the requisite piercing arrows.

The pool was drained. I cried fit to fill it with tears.

I had loved that house and the life that we lived within it. But—here was where it was *almost* marvelous—try as I would, I could not love the rhythms of suburban life; they simply did not mesh with my metabolism, and in the decade that we lived there, I never stopped floating in day-dreams in which we were living in Manhattan, and think-ing, If I could just have this man in this marriage in that town, I would have everything that I could ever want in life.

I even believed it.

And then it happened.

We had recently returned from a work vacation in Haiti.

We had spent several of his vacations there, in the poor-est part of the poorest country in the Western Hemisphere, where Hal would work in a hospital carved out of jungle: Hôpital Albert Schweitzer in the village of Deschapelles, in the Artibonite Valley.

The peasants would come swarming down from their mountain huts, sometimes days away, carrying their sick on litters, or in their arms, and he would find himself practicing not just urology but neurology, cardiology, orthopedics, obstetrics, anything that had to be done.

I watched him perform a delivery once. He had to do a cesarean. I averted my gaze from the cut, then turned back to see my husband's hand reach into the depths of this young woman and pull out, by God, a baby. Doctor and patient grinned at each other, joined in a moment more intimate, in its way, than any he and I could ever share.

He asked his nurse for the patient's name. "Cecile," the nurse said. He said, "Tell Cecile she has a beautiful son." Then the new mother whispered something, and the nurse said, "She's asking your name, Doctor."

So somewhere amid those thatched-roof huts, if he has managed to survive the hurricanes and the cholera and the unspeakable, unrelievable poverty, is a man named Harold Alexander Lear Pouissant.

Hal would come back from those trips exhausted but exhilarated, feeling closer, he often said, to the moral core of his profession than he ever felt at home.

We had just returned from Deschapelles when he said one day, "I want more."

"More what?"

"More usefulness. A more useful kind of medicine than you can do in one-on-one private practice."

He found it in the relatively new field of community medicine. His beloved old hospital in Manhattan ran a community-medicine department that served a huge local population, many of whose residents lived below the poverty line. The need was great. The department would be glad to have him.

"You understand," he said, "that would mean moving back to New York. That okay with you?"

He was smiling.

I was ecstatic.

Yet another variation on the old beware-of-dreams-that-come-true theme.

It was bad from the beginning.

Promises had been made that were not kept.

He wanted to develop programs. Ample funding had been assured. It was not forthcoming.

He had envisioned community medicine as a noble

calling. It turned out to be a pit of politics and moneygrubbing instead.

He managed, nonetheless, to develop a direly needed sex-education program, both for medical students and within the community. And then, after it had grown hugely successful, getting publicity for the hospital, becoming a model for such projects in hospitals all across the country, the program was taken away from him.

This program really should be run by a psychiatrist, said the Department of Psychiatry.

Run by a psychiatrist? But it's my program, he said.

You can assist him, said the Department of Psychiatry.

But how can you take away my program? he said.

Sorry, said the Department of Psychiatry.

That was when he had his first heart attack. His heart's way, I suppose, of saying, You can't fire me; I quit.

Then there was another heart attack, and another, and open-heart surgery, from which he emerged with brain damage, his recent memory shot to hell, stumbling around in a kind of premature senility of which he was totally aware and which for him was immeasurably worse than any physical disability, and from then on it was a downward trajectory, and he knew that, too. Never stopped fighting it, but knew it all the way.

I believe that in moments of crisis, just as in normal aging, most of us become more of whatever we were to begin with. (Live long enough, and we become, in reliable ways, caricatures of ourselves.) He had always had grace. In terminal illness, he was an astonishment of grace.

"I don't need you hovering around here handing me pills. I need to see you getting on with your life," he said one day, in that labored way that his voice was coming out by then. He lay propped high in the bed, oxygen prongs in his nose, oxygen tank at his bedside, the wheelchair, in which I had so often wheeled him, now parked in a corner from which it was rarely moved. "You're always bitching about how the men writers have those bars where they can get together and yak after a day's work, and the women don't have anyplace. Why don't you start something for the women?"

(I did, in fact, call a few women writer friends, and we started a writers' group. The designated subject was work, but we quickly morphed into more of a consciousness-raising group, sharing the most intimate confidences, which was the way the wind blew back then. Recently, we began meeting again. Now we have grown children, grandchildren, complicated family lives, all sorts of intimate matters we could discuss, but we don't. We discuss our work, which is the way the wind blows now.)

And then, in that final phase, when his doctors had stepped back because they could not confront their own helplessness, a new doctor—young, just out of training—came into his life one night in the emergency room.

That was Stuart, who would stick with him through those last several months, until the end, which came almost five years after it had begun.

Stuart, who sat now by my bedside and said, "Still ghosts? Even after all this time, Martha?"

Oh, yes, Stuart. Even after all this time. Who ever declared an expiration date on ghosts?

chapter thirteen

I want to go home, I said.

Of course you do. Just two more weeks, the social worker said.

But I can walk now, I said.

Barely, she said. (Which was true.) And you still need intensive physiotherapy. You have to finish the course.

What for?

For everything. Can you walk up and down flights of steps? Can you put on your shoes and socks? Can you get into a bathtub? Can you cook a meal? Can you walk to your kitchen without a walker? Can you walk there *with* a walker and fill a kettle with water and set it on a burner and walk to a cabinet and reach up for a cup and carry it to the kettle and pour a cup of tea and carry it to the table?

No, to all the above. My own weakness astonished me.

Well then, she said.

But *I'm* home, Al said. She doesn't have to do any of those things. I can do them for her.

But the antibiotic treatment is still going on and it must be completed, the social worker said.

Why? She is obviously getting better, Al said.

So we can be sure the infection is gone.

Oh? So now you know that's what made her leg go bad? The infection?

Well, whatever it was. I'm not a doctor.

It was not clear that I would be admitted to the hospital's physiotherapy program. "They take only the very bad stuff," the social worker said. "They may decide that you're not bad enough."

We waited to hear. It was like waiting to hear whether you've been admitted to some exclusive club, and hoping that they turn you down.

They took me. It was not simply my weakness but the

double whammy of a potentially fatal infection on the heels of a substantial heart attack, one of them said, that made me "bad enough" to be admitted.

That was their view of it. My own view of it, as I began working to recover strengths that were blessedly recoverable amid other patients who were less blessed, with their shattered limbs, their broken necks, their injured spinal cords—and most of them in remarkably stoic spirits—was that I was healthy and in the wrong place. I felt self-conscious, like a slim person sitting amid the overweight in a Weight Watchers class.

"You didn't have any idea," one of the therapists said to me later, "how fragile you were."

Every other day I was taken down into a subbasement of the building, to begin relearning how to cope with what the social worker had called, appropriately enough, *normal life.*

Down there was a whole other world. Down there was a series of units—little theatrical sets, I thought of them—constructed true to scale.

A model shower stall, where I would be taught how to navigate a four-inch-high threshold suddenly transformed into an Alp and to grip the safety bar while setting myself down gingerly upon a shower stool.

A model bathroom, where I would learn how to maintain my balance at the sink and how to sit on a standard-height toilet seat.

A model of the front half of an automobile, where I would practice releasing the walker and easing myself backward into the passenger seat.

A model kitchen, furnished down to every mundane detail, where I would learn how to perform the remarkably numerous steps involved in preparing a cup of tea while negotiating a walker.

Who would have dreamed how hard it could be to perform these simple tasks? That was the revelation.

I was being moved to a room in the physiotherapy unit. On moving day, several of the nurses and aides came by to wish me well. The aide Sam said, "I'll visit you." I said, "Oh, please do," knowing that he wouldn't. (A week later, he did. "How are they treating you here? You in good hands with Allstate?" he asked.)

Now I had company: a roommate who was obviously in great pain from knee-replacement surgery—performed, I gathered, in a different hospital—that was not healing properly. She was very heavy, which made it worse. And she had a bad heart, she told me, and diabetes as well. But she was of such an open, jolly nature that it seemed nothing could subdue her.

"Oh, my, look at you go, you're walking so *good!*" she would say, her hand fixed like a carapace upon the grossly swollen knee. "Pretty soon now you'll be able to throw out that walker!"

My own visitors came in ones and twos, and mostly by day. Hers came in the evenings—six, eight, or more at a time. She had a huge, boisterous family, and they made plenty of noise and lingered well past the good-night bell, all against house rules, but were such a friendly bunch, so kind to me—*How you doing tonight, hon? Water? Can I get you more water?*—that I never wanted to complain.

When they departed, the good-byes, which never varied, took on the cadence of a churchly call-and-response:

"Love you, Mama!"

"Love you more!"

"Love you, Grandma!"

"Love you more!"

We traded confidences. I grew fond of her. One morning, when I awoke, she was gone. I asked about her but was never told anything, except wordlessly by a young aide, who gave me a thumbs-down.

I still think of her sometimes. Something in the nature

of that call-and-response that seems to me primal and crucial:

Love you, Mama!

Love you more!

They agreed to spring me for Thanksgiving.

Al's children, Julie and David, and David's wife and daughters, who lived just outside Boston—all of us would be gathering on Central Park West, in the apartment last seen when I had said to Al five weeks earlier, light-years earlier, "Of *course* we'll be able to go to Charleston tomorrow!"

I was unsteady with excitement. My hands trembled so that I couldn't fasten my buttons. An aide had to help me dress. Another wheeled me down to the entrance lobby. Al wheeled me out to the car, where David waited, and I maneuvered myself—rear first, as I had been taught—into the passenger seat, and we took off for the West Side, three people traveling a scant mile on an ordinary road in an ordinary way. For the strangeness of it, I might have been traveling in a rocket to the moon.

Huge hellos from the building staff. Of course they all knew where I had been, and why I had been there; there is no grapevine more efficient than the one that operates amid the staff of a Manhattan co-op apartment building.

Al wheeled me through the foyer, into the elevator, and out onto the sixth-floor landing. The door to the apartment opened and there they were, all those grinning faces, and I made my Big Entrance: Got out of the chair and walked a few steps *sans* walker.

Great round of applause. I, in heaven. At the table, many toasts. It was as joyous a Thanksgiving dinner as I could recall, and I could recall many. Thanksgiving is twin to Christmas in this way. You can't help recalling Thanksgivings past: faces added, faces gone, tweakings of pleasure and pain.

I remembered those in the house in West Hartford, when Hal and I had both been young and strong and I could prepare the holiday meal for a couple of dozen guests without help and almost without blinking; and one Thanksgiving, a decade later, when he lay in the Intensive Care Unit here in New York and I sat with his children by his bedside, willing the gods to give us reason to say thanks, which, on that occasion, they did; and the first one after he died, when my brother, Joe, and I passed on the turkey and went downtown to order corned-beef sandwiches at Stage Deli instead; and many Thanksgivings of various mood colors in the years that followed, sometimes deeply blue, sometimes rosy, sometimes, as I came fully back into the world, in the company of one man or another; and the first Thanksgiving weekend with Al, quite soon after we had met, which we spent in a little cottage at the edge of a lake on Cape Cod, hot and shy with each other.

After dinner, I took the walker and ventured over to our picture gallery, that long hallway leading to the bedroom, its walls lined on either side with the pictures, scores upon scores of pictures that reflect back to us the story of ourselves. Al and his late wife, Judy, from their separate childhoods through their shared grandparenthood; and Hal and I through all our own life stages; and then Al and I in the story we had lived thus far; and all our parents and even some of our grandparents, the earliest in sepia, all facing one another on the walls.

Amid these ghosts of the past, my own ghosts began to rise up again.

I remembered when my stepdaughter, Judith, had telephoned me just days after Hal had died. She had been suffering the loss of him terribly. That day, sounding elated, she had told me: "I had the most wonderful dream last night. I dreamed that Dad was flying up in the sky. He

was his old healthy self. He was wearing a Superman cos-
tume, and guess what was written on the front of it? Your
telephone number! And he gave me that big grin and said,
'Don't worry, Judy. You can always call me.'"

I remembered how I had felt his presence, in those first
months after he was gone, and how it had given me the
sense that I was not diminished by his death but somehow
stronger and wiser than before, being now not just myself,
but the sum of all that we had been together.

I remembered how I had been able to summon up that
voice, a voice that was neither his nor mine but the sum
of our pooled best instincts, and how comforting it had
been—how, when I had said, *Today the loss of you hurts too
much to bear, what should I do?* the voice had said, *Go to a
movie*, which had turned out to be splendid advice; and
how, when I had said once, *I don't want to end up living in
your bathrobe*, the voice had said, *Then choose not to*—also
precisely what I had needed to hear.

And now, suddenly, rising up out of my imagination—
or out of my blood, for I had never been sure of the difference—that sense of presence came back to me. I stood
gazing at those faces—five generations up there on the
walls, three generations gathered at the Thanksgiving table

nearby, with the two granddaughters budding like flowers, promise of all that might yet be—and I heard that inner voice that had always cleared my mind by cutting straight to the chase.

Continuity, it said.

And the ghosts lay down to rest.

acknowledgments

Briefly, but deeply felt, my thanks to the following specialists, all of whom are supremely good at their various crafts.

Dr. Sanford J. Friedman

Dr. David Seinfeld

Dr. Timothy J. Harkin

Gloria Loomis, my agent and cherished friend, and her wonderful young colleague Julia Masnik

Jane Friedman, Tina Pohlman, Rachel Chou, Jack Palmer, Sakina Esufally, and all those helpful, eager, supersmart people at Open Road Media who treat writers and books with a respect that makes working with them a joy.

about the author

Martha Weinman Lear is the author of *Where Did I Leave My Glasses?* as well as the bestsellers *The Child Worshipers* and *Heartsounds*, which became a Peabody Award–winning film. She is a former articles editor and staff writer for the *New York Times Magazine* and has written extensively for that and many other national publications, including *AARP The Magazine*, the *New Yorker*, the *New York Times Book Review*, *GQ*, *House Beautiful*, *Redbook*, *Ladies' Home Journal*, *Woman's Day*, *McCall's*, *Family Circle*, and *Reader's Digest*, often on medical, cultural, and sociological subjects. She lives in New York City with her husband, screenwriter Albert Ruben.

EBOOKS BY
MARTHA WEINMAN LEAR

FROM OPEN ROAD MEDIA

 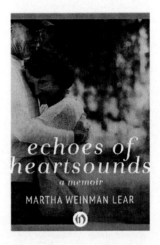

Available wherever ebooks are sold

INTEGRATED MEDIA

Open Road Integrated Media is a digital publisher and multimedia content company. Open Road creates connections between authors and their audiences by marketing its ebooks through a new proprietary online platform, which uses premium video content and social media.

Videos, Archival Documents, and New Releases

Sign up for the Open Road Media newsletter and get news delivered straight to your inbox.

Sign up now at
www.openroadmedia.com/newsletters

CPSIA information can be obtained at www.ICGtesting.com
Printed in the USA
LVOW12s1308300814

401630LV00002B/70/P